The Heirs of Jane Austen

American University Studies

Series IV
English Language and Literature

Vol. 180

PETER LANG
New York • Washington, D.C./Baltimore
Bern • Frankfurt am Main • Berlin • Vienna • Paris

Rachel R. Mather

√The Heirs of Jane Austen

Twentieth-Century Writers of the Comedy of Manners

PETER LANG
New York • Washington, D.C./Baltimore
Bern • Frankfurt am Main • Berlin • Vienna • Paris

Library of Congress Cataloging-in-Publication Data

Mather, Rachel R.
The heirs of Jane Austen: twentieth-century writers
of the comedy of manners/ Rachel R. Mather.
   p. cm. — (American university studies.
Series IV, English language and literature; vol. 180)
Includes bibliographical references and index.
1. English fiction—20th century—History and criticism. 2. Manners and
customs in literature. 3. Benson, E.F. (Edward Frederic), 1867–1940—
Criticism and interpretation. 4. Delafield, E.M., 1890–1943—Criticism and
interpretation. 5. Thirkell, Angela Mackail, 1890–1961—Criticism and
interpretation. 6. Austen, Jane, 1775–1817—Influence. 7. Literature and
society—England—History—20th century. 8. Women in literature.
9. Humorous stories, English—History and criticism. I. Title. II. Series.
   PR888.S615M38   823'.9109355—dc20   96-124
              ISBN 0-8204-2624-5
              ISSN 0741-0700

Die Deutsche Bibliothek-CIP-Einheitsaufnahme

Mather, Rachel R.:
The heirs of Jane Austen: twentieth-century writers of the
comedy of manners/ Rachel R. Mather. –New York; Washington,
D.C./Baltimore; Bern; Frankfurt am Main; Berlin; Vienna; Paris: Lang.
   (American university studies: Ser. 4,
   English language and literature; Vol. 180)
              ISBN 0-8204-2624-5
NE: American university studies/ 04

To
My Children

Melissa, Walter, Rebecca, Nancy
Nathaniel, Jeremiah, Abigail, Timothy, and Daisy
for their steadfast interest
and involvement

&

Contents

Acknowledgments

This work evolved through my mother and father's value for education. I had become very interested in E. M. Delafield upon being introduced to her Provincial Lady Diaries by "Miss Read" (Dora Jessie Saint), whose work with the light essay so much resembles that of Delafield.

I am fortunate to have had steady support and encouragement on this project since its inception as a research essay written with the guidance of the English Department at St. John's University. The questions and views on Jane Austen of my mentor, Professor Veronica M. S. Kennedy, have provided me with new insight into social satire, and her reflections on conditions in England during World War II have reinforced my appreciation of Angela Thirkell's created world as social history.

I have been fortunate in being able to count on true buddies Nancy Davis, Irene Miller, Carol Mylod, and Mary Russo as patient listeners and believers forever.

For opening windows, I thank my daughter Abby Salamin, a Thirkell fan, who looks with the fresh eye of a new generation at Thirkell's traditional view of women.

Special thanks to my sister Karin Williams for her clear-eyed approach that has made the book more accessible to those meeting the twentieth-century comedy of manners writers for the first time.

The manuscript has benefitted from trusted colleague Craig Ash's meticulous comments on the Jane Austen material and from generous friend Mildred Carter's painstaking copyediting.

Sr. Gladys Mary, C.H.N., who also had first-hand experience of the war years in England, reminded me that the "kitchen" and the "dining room" of the Thirkell wartime novels held inherently different attitudes towards food rationing. Gerard Woodcock, another "Janeite," sent me the English advertisements for the books on Jane Austen and food before they were available here.

I am grateful to Heidi Burns, Acquisitions Editor at Peter Lang Publishing, for piloting me through this book. It is a stronger work for her help and encouragement.

I am forever indebted to artist Elizabeth Doran for going beyond the call of duty in enhancing the text and endlessly accommodating doubt on felicitous wording.

Permissions Acknowledgments

Grateful acknowledgment is made to the publishers who have granted permission to reprint excerpts from previously published material:

Thirkell, Angela, *August Folly*. New York: Alfred A. Knopf, 1936. Reprinted by permission of Alfred A. Knopf/Random House.

Thirkell, Angela, *Before Lunch*. New York: Alfred A. Knopf, 1940. Reprinted by permission of Alfred A. Knopf/Random House.

Extract from "Letter to Lord Byron," in *Collected Poems*, copyright 1936, by W. H. Auden. Reprinted by permission of Random House.

Auden, W. H., extract of five lines from "Letter to Lord Byron," *Collected Poems*, edited by Edward Mendelson. Faber & Faber, Ltd., London, 1988. Reprinted by permission of the publisher.

List of Abbreviations

Page references to Jane Austen's novels and letters are given in the text. The editions and abbreviations used are as follows:

The Novels of Jane Austen, ed. R. W. Chapman (London: Oxford UP, 1965)

E	*Emma*
MP	*Mansfield Park*
NA	*Northanger Abbey*
P	*Persuasion*
P&P	*Pride and Prejudice*
S&S	*Sense and Sensibility*

L *Jane Austen's Letters*, ed. R. W. Chapman (London: Oxford UP, 1979)

Page references to E. F. Benson's novels and informal autobiography are given in the text. The abbreviations used are as follows:

LL	*Lucia in London*
M&L	*Mapp and Lucia*
MM	*Miss Mapp*
QL	*Queen Lucia*
TFL	*Trouble for Lucia*
TWL	*The Worshipful Lucia*
FE	*Final Edition: Informal Autobiography* (London: Longmans, 1940).

Page references to E. M. Delafield's Provincial Lady Diaries
are given in the text. The abbreviations used are as follows:

DPL   *The Diary of a Provincial Lady*
PLL   *The Provincial Lady in London*
PLA   *The Provincial Lady in America*
PLW   *The Provincial Lady in Wartime*

Page references to Angela Thirkell's novels are given in the
text. The abbreviations used are as follows:

AF   *August Folly*
BL   *Before Lunch*
CBI   *Cheerfulness Breaks In*
GU   *Growing Up*
HR   *High Rising*
MB   *Miss Bunting*
MH   *Marling Hall*
NR   *Northbridge Rectory*
PT   *Pomfret Towers*
SH   *Summer Half*
TB   *The Brandons*
TH   *The Headmistress*
WS   *Wild Strawberries*

Introduction

The influence of Jane Austen (1775–1817) on George Eliot and Henry James was acknowledged by the writers themselves, as well as by their contemporaries, and her influence on E. M. Forster's early novels has been demonstrated in a modern critical study.[1] In the mid-twentieth century, reviewers saw the novels of Barbara Pym and, more recently, the early novels of Anita Brookner, as following in the Jane Austen tradition. Has the contemporary reader lost sight of what the Jane Austen tradition means? The Jane Austen tradition means the *comedy of manners*. This is the name given to a dramatic and literary form dating from Greek and Roman dramatists, popular during Restoration comedy and again in Edwardian novels, that deals with "relations and intrigues of men and women living in a polished and sophisticated society, relying for comic effect in great part on the wit and sparkle of the dialogue."[2] Three noteworthy modern English comic writers, E. F. Benson, for his Lucia novels (published between 1920–1939), E. M. Delafield, for her Provincial Lady novels (published between 1930–1941), and Angela Thirkell, for her early Barsetshire novels (1934–1945), merit a critical review that will show how they exemplify the Jane Austen tradition in their novels.

To establish Jane Austen in the comedy of manners tradition, critic Ian Watt portrays her as the heir of eighteenth-century author Fanny Burney, following both Samuel Richardson, "in a minute presentation of daily life" as shown in *Sir Charles Grandison*, and Henry Fielding, "in evaluating (her material) from a comic and objective point of view."[3] For the past three decades, however, literary criticism has come into its own as a separate and significant art, and with critical analysis illuminating the Jane Austen novels not only in meaning, language, and structure, but also style, there has been some rethinking of her place in the comedy of manners. Without prejudice to Jane Austen's role as a didactic novelist, literary critics Harold Bloom and Jan Fergus both represent modern critical views that establish a line distinct from that of Fanny Burney. Bloom denies the influence of Fielding, arguing that Jane Austen is the daughter of Richardson as she is the "ancestor of George Eliot and Henry James rather than of Dickens and Thackeray"; that her "own moral and spiritual concerns fuse in the crucial need of her heroines to sustain their individual integrities, a need so intense that it compels them to fall into those errors about life that are necessary (to experience) life" fully; and that these heroines "follow, though in a comic register," Richardson's tragic Clarissa Harlowe.[4] To distinguish Jane Austen from her predecessors, Fergus suggests that in *Pride and Prejudice* Austen adapts and expands the eighteenth-century tradition of the comedy of manners in the novel, that Richardson and Burney used but did not develop.[5]

The elements of the Jane Austen tradition include *wit* and *dialogue*, which for Austen are separate terms: for example, Mr. Bennet's outbursts of witticism, used to foreclose dialogue[6]; *a minute presentation of daily life*, or the well-known recommendation of Jane Austen in a letter to her niece Anna Austen that "3 or 4 Families in a Country Village is the very thing to work on" (*L* 100 401); and *comic register*, including irony. What makes her different from her predecessors is her *social satire*, which Fergus describes as "merciless; it admits no extenuation; but it is not misanthropy."[7] It is without malice or preaching, or what Horace termed "chastising through humor."[8] Earlier, Virginia Woolf casts a brilliant light on what she characterizes as Jane Austen's "elusive quality": "She wishes neither to reform nor to annihilate . . . . She encircles (her characters) with the lash of a whip-like phrase which, as it runs round them, cuts out their silhouettes for ever . . . . No touch of pettiness, no hint of spite, rouses us from our contemplation. Delight strangely mingles with our amusement."[9]

We find that this tradition, its focus on the relationship of the heroine to society, was later carried forward by Elizabeth Gaskell in *Cranford* (1853), forming the link between Jane Austen and the twentieth-century writers Benson, Delafield, and Thirkell. *Cranford* has a more "gentle humour" of "the narrative of daily incident and custom,"[10] connected with the "elegant economy" of the secure little group. The "Amazons" of Cranford are in the same social class, but there is little money except what is attributed to the Honorable Mrs. Jamieson at the top, and that which is more generously shown by Miss Betty Barker, a former ladies'-maid now accepted as a social equal, at the other end. *Cranford* has, in fact, become one of the touchstones of feminist reference, its unified society demonstrating supportive sisterhood. Critic Edgar Wright suggests that Gaskell is more of an "ironical observer"[11] than a social satirist, an appropriate example being the narrator Mary Smith's comment on the difference between her father as a businessman and the unworldly Miss Matty Jenkyns:

> But my father says 'such simplicity might be very well in Cranford, but would never do in the world.' And I fancy the world must be very bad, for with all my father's suspicion of every one with whom he has dealings, and in spite of all his many precautions, he lost upwards of a thousand pounds by roguery only last year. (*Cranford* 174)

Cranford's humor, tone, and village setting link Jane Austen and the twentieth-century writers of the domestic comedy of manners.

In the field of Jane Austen criticism, a continuing scholarly issue is *mastery of character*; that is, whether her characters "enjoy a continuing existence in the reader's imagination, free of the page."[12]   According to J. B. Priestley, "Jane Austen only once achieved poetry and that was when (*P&P*) she created Mr. Collins." He is "a Romantic," "a man apart," and "the happiest creature in the book . . . . He comes into Hertfordshire . . . as if he were entering fairyland."[13]

> Although we feel that we know what he will do and say next, yet he always goes beyond our expectations just as absurd people in real life do; we know the kind of thing he will say, yet we could not say it for him (as we could with a lesser comic character), for his absurdity is always a little in advance of what we can possibly imagine . . . he does not exist simply for the sake of the story (though he plays his part in it) . . . but exists in his own right and compels his creator to indulge him all over the place.[14]

However, in his 1976 rethinking on the English comic character, Priestley finds that Jane Austen has been too indulgent with Mr. Collins, that "feminine" humor is ordinarily less indulgent than masculine humor. Humor needs irony, affection, and contact with reality. Feminine humor is more often characterized by "light, satirical wit"; it "makes a much better job of these little intimate meetings," which make up so much of the domestic comedy of manners " . . . (with its) pretensions, dubious motives . . . and social absurdities."[15] The modern literary critic might find it dangerous to agree that there are different qualities in masculine and feminine humor. Nonetheless, Priestley includes irony and satirical wit as humor. He also describes elements of the subgenre *domestic comedy of manners*, the term most appropriate to link Gaskell, then Benson, Delafield, and Thirkell with Jane Austen.

When establishing a line from Jane Austen through Elizabeth Gaskell to these three writers, one must distinguish between tradition and influence. We have no reason to suppose that Benson, Delafield, or Thirkell consciously set out to write in a way that follows Jane Austen, even though their novels include the three or four families in a country village. Collected criticism of Jane Austen indicates that many readers of the time had read her novels.

In his informal autobiography, *Final Edition*, Benson demonstrates not only awareness of Jane Austen but a testimonial to kinship with her. He makes an ongoing analogy between his admired friend, Lady Sandhurst, and Jane Austen that implicitly defines how he sees the writer: "(Lady Sandhurst) had the genuine Jane Austen eye . . . she saw with that uniquely humourous perception, and never omitted to turn its kindly but ironical searchlight on herself" (224). *Uniquely humourous perception* and *kindly but ironical searchlight* characterize Jane Austen's art, serve to relate Lady Sandhurst to Jane Austen, and identify Benson's own Jane Austen eye for a kindred soul. His account of one of Lady Sandhurst's parties provides us not only with the reality of the choreography, which now makes social history, of the formal dinner parties of the Benson, Delafield, and Thirkell novels, but also with a vivid picture of the ritual of after-dinner coffee at Longbourn (*P&P*) that effectively prevents Elizabeth and Darcy from talking to each other upon their first meeting after the Lydia episode:

> . . . this party (was) pure Jane Austen: we went down to dinner arm-in-arm, and the men talked to their partners on the right till about the time they had eaten their fish, and then taking advantage of a pause they turned to the lady on the left . . . . Afterwards, when the men joined the ladies again upstairs we found them sitting in a group together, but on our entry they opened out like a fan and the men inserted themselves in vacant places, and engaged in dialogues . . . . But nobody had enjoyed it more than Jane Austen: she had been making notes all the time for some chapter in a book of hers which, alas, seems to be out of print. (227)

There is no need to surmise from this affectionate portrayal that Benson set out to write in the style of Jane Austen. To what extent did her style influence him? He came from a cultured and literary family; they all wrote. Even before he attended King's College at Cambridge University, he and his sister wrote the family's "Saturday Magazine," and in 1893 his Dodo novels had already made him famous. Benson is, in fact, the only one of the three modern authors to have had a university education. Delafield, too, came from a cultured and literary background. Her mother was a prolific writer of novels and plays. Delafield wrote her first novel towards the end of World War II. In the Provincial Lady novels, Delafield makes only one reference to Jane Austen: The Provincial Lady is embarking on a trip abroad and has received unsatisfactory answers to her query to her family and neighbors as to what books she should take along. The Provincial Lady notes: "Finally decide on *Little Dorrit* and (Charlotte Yonge's) *The Daisy Chain*, with *Jane Eyre* in coat-pocket. Should prefer to be the kind of person who is inseparable from volume of Keats, or even Jane Austen, but cannot compass this" (*DPL* 211). In short, her persona's tastes in literature are not low-brow, but Keats and Jane Austen are on a higher plane.

Priestley's analysis of the memorable comic character applies as much to the Provincial Lady as to Jane Austen's Mr. Collins: that "(she) goes beyond our expectations just as absurd people in real life do" and "we know the kind of thing (she) will say, yet we could not say it for (her) (as we could with a lesser comic character)."[16] Delafield created two other strong comic characters in Robert, the Provincial Lady's husband, and Old Mrs. Blenkinsop, with her perpetual martyrdom that causes the Provincial Lady to "reach home totally unbenefited by this visit, and with strange tendency to snap at everybody I meet" (*DPL* 102), but the Provincial Lady herself is the unforgettable "modest, fumbling, but curiously dry-witted heroine."[17]

There is no question that the third author meant to write in a literary, referential style. Angela Thirkell's authorial language reflects her wide reading, education, and culture. She was a granddaughter of Edward Burne-Jones, daughter of Professor George Mackail, and sister of *Greenery Street* novelist Denis Mackail, and cousin of Rudyard Kipling. At times her novels purposefully feature both oblique and overt references to the fictional worlds of Jane Austen, as well as of Anthony Trollope, Dickens, and others, associations that the knowledgeable reader joyfully recognizes.

It is the dual purpose of literature to give pleasure and to teach. The comedy of manners has given pleasure to generations of readers. Jane Austen's novels have been enjoyed for the very reason that the characters are "timeless"; they are not dated by their speech and clothing; and it is a truth universally and forever acknowledged that a single man in possession of a good fortune must be in want of a wife. Scholars have established that Jane Austen worked with a calendar; the significant dates in her novels coincide with the days of the week in a particular year. She is known to have been so precise about authenticity that she asked her sister, Cassandra, if she "could discover whether Northamptonshire is a country of Hedgerows" (*L* 76 298), for the projected setting of *Mansfield Park.* These are more than the techniques of a creative writer; the elements of the domestic comedy of manners as Jane Austen infused them with the story of her characters add up to a social history of her time.

In addition, one learns from the conventions of irony and the comedy of manners. Jane Austen is not limited to the comedy of manners, for modern critical views have established and developed her moral purpose. She can do both, and one can learn from her didactic novels; still, it would be one-sided to identify her as a moralist. Benson, Delafield, and Thirkell are direct heirs of the Jane Austen tradition, and their novels give a great deal of pleasure as well as instruction in the literary conventions of irony and the comedy of manners.

That pleasure was borne out by their immediate popularity: Benson's Lucia novels had a cult following, including Noel Coward and Gertrude Lawrence, and in 1932 the *Daily Mail* Ideal Home Exhibition had a Mapp & Lucia garden. Delafield's *The Diary of a Provincial Lady* was first published in installments in 1930 and in book form a year later; and Thirkell's *The Brandons* was a 1939 choice of the Book of the Month Club. Then, with the seriousness of the war effort and the deaths of both Benson, in 1939, and Delafield, in 1943, their novels suffered an eclipse. Humor was no longer taken as seriously or received as enthusiastically as it had been before World War II, nor has irony crossed the Atlantic successfully. These novels have not become classics in the subgenre, although they merit this status. This dilemma, in terms of *The Diary of a Provincial Lady*, has been called "the conundrum of an unknown classic."[18]

With the cyclical surge of reissuing their novels in paperback in the 1980s, all three twentieth-century authors have received public notice—all the more reason for a reappraisal and appreciation of the humor, the irony, the social satire, and the social history in these novels. With some variation in emphasis, their topics are those of the Jane Austen novels: the heroines in relation to society; clergymen, a major ingredient of the domestic comedy of manners; and the social history of village life. In addition, their language, "light, and bright, and sparkling" with verbal irony, metonymy, and synecdoche, reflects the Jane Austen style. Through individual treatments of the topics common to the novels, Benson, Delafield, and Thirkell can be distinguished within the tradition in a way that is meaningful to the contemporary reader. The significance of the woman writer's experiences should not be overlooked. This modern feminine interest can be found in the Delafield Provincial Lady novels in particular and, more lightly, in the writing persona of Angela Thirkell in her Barsetshire novels. While one can hardly make a similar claim for Benson, his rendering of Lucia and her self-dramatization is the epitome of the wit and confusions of her era.

1

E. F. Benson

When life becomes too much for us we shall be able
to take refuge in the giardino segretto.[1]

Edward F. Benson, like many of his contemporaries, was a great
admirer of Jane Austen, illustrating critic B. C. Southam's statement
that well-read people read the novels and had opinions on them. In fact, it
is difficult to overstate how *in fashion* the novels of Jane Austen were during
the second half of the nineteenth century and the beginning of the twentieth,
particularly after the publication, in 1870, of the *Memoir* by her nephew J.
A. Austen-Leigh. At the same time, Southam makes it clear that one must
recognize that there was a second school of thought, represented by
Charlotte Brontë, who, after reading *Emma*, wrote to her editor in April
1850 that she found there "nothing more than a delineation of 'the surface of
the lives of genteel English people'" and Jane Austen herself "a complete and
most sensible lady, but a very incomplete, and rather insensible (*not
senseless*) woman."[2] In 1896, when Charlotte Brontë's letter appeared in
print, Joseph Jacobs, editor of an 1896 illustrated edition of *Emma*, wrote in
his Introduction that those opinions were "unjust."

Southam's collection of the comments, judgments, and criticism of the
novels from Jane Austen's death in 1816 until the 1940s does not include the
growing body of critical analysis of her work, literary theory having only
recently, that is, since the 1940s, become an independent scholarly field. It
is important to note that these literary critics have made it clear that Jane
Austen is not to be limited by the comedy of manners and have established
her as a didactic novelist.

Nevertheless, the popularity of her novels at the time means that the
young Benson, from a literary family and milieu, would be at least as

familiar with them as an ardent young reader today might be with Charlotte Brontë's *Jane Eyre* or George Eliot's *Middlemarch*, both touchstones of the feminist canon, and probably more familiar, judging by his describing Lady Sandhurst, his long-time and much admired friend, as "Jane Austen." Benson reveals his affinity for Jane Austen and for the Jane Austen tradition, which, when he wrote the Lucia novels, meant the comedy of manners, in his attribution to Lady Sandhurst of some of those characteristics that he sees in Jane Austen as a writer: "alertness," "the receptiveness and the elasticity which are the essential qualities of youth," and the quality of "thrilled interest" (*FE* 232,4). *Thrilled interest* recalls Jane Austen's intense interest in the details of daily life as recorded in one of her letters to her sister, Cassandra: "You know how interesting the purchase of a spongecake is to me" (*L*100 401). His final words on Lady Sandhurst's traditionally formal birthday party, "But nobody had enjoyed it more than Jane Austen: she had been making notes all the time for some chapter in a book of hers which, alas, seems to be out of print" (*FE* 238), evokes a picture of Jane Austen drawn by her niece Marianne Knight:

> Aunt Jane would sit quietly working beside the fire in the library, saying nothing for a good while, and then would suddenly burst out laughing, jump up and run across the room to a table where pens and paper were lying, write something down, and then come back to the fire and go on quietly working as before.[3]

A further illustration of his link with Jane Austen, one that gives insight into the nature of the creative process, is Benson's account of how he came to write about Tilling and Miss Mapp. He was then living in Rye, in Henry James' Lamb House, identified in the novels as Mallards:

> what a setting, I thought, Rye and its cobbled streets and its gables and red brick . . . would make for some fantastic story! . . . . As an external observer I had seen the ladies of Rye doing their shopping in the High Street every morning, carrying large market baskets, and finding a great deal to say to each other . . . . I outlined an elderly atrocious spinster and established her in Lamb House. She should be the centre of social life, abhorred and dominant, and she should sit like a great spider behind the curtains in the garden-room, spying on her friends, and I knew her name must be Elizabeth Mapp. Rye should furnish

the typography [sic], and this should be the busy little town called Tilling . . .
Perhaps another preposterous woman, Lucia of Riseholme, who already had a
decent and devout following, and who was as dominant as Mapp, might come
into contact with her some day, when I got to know Mapp better. I began to
invent a new set of characters who should revolve around these two women,
fussy and eager and alert and preposterous . . . jealousies and malignities and
devouring inquisitiveness. (*FE* 171)

This, then, is the tradition Benson works in: Jane Austen laughing as
she makes a note; his observing, with that *thrilled interest* and the *kindly but
ironical* eye with which Jane Austen observed her heroines, the gatherings
in the High Street of Rye to create his stories of Tilling. Stephen Pile, a
current Benson scholar, delineates his style within the tradition in a way that
doubtless is not inaccurate, but which emphasizes the *jealousies and
malignities and devouring inquisitiveness* without conveying the humor that
most critics before Pile have attributed to the Lucia novels:

Benson's distinctive vision of provincial England, riddled with malice and
snobbery, where correct form is all . . . . Appearances are everything and
society functions through an harmonious system of mutual insincerities. The
characters lie to themselves and others, being deluded in the rare moments when
not gossiping.[4]

While this description also fits Jane Austen's characters Miss Bingley
and Mrs. Hurst (*P&P*), as well as Mrs. John Dashwood and her mother,
Mrs. Ferrars, and Lucy and Anne Steele (*S&S*), and this satire contributes
to the humor, those characters are not the heart of the novels, as Lucia and
her circle are.

*"None of them could be described as estimable, and they are certainly not
very interesting, yet they are fascinated by each other and we are
fascinated by them."*[5]

Criticism of the Lucia novels may be expected to vary, according not
only to the reviewer, but to the times. In the Introduction to the 1936
omnibus edition of the novels, Gilbert Seldes describes them as "the most
enchantingly malicious works written by the hand of man." He also claims

that they are a "triumph of art over life, because although I feel I would do almost anything to avoid meeting either Lucia or Miss Mapp in person, I have gone to considerable pain to meet them again and again in the novels which Mr. Benson has written about them."[6]

Over almost twenty years some variation of this phrase was also applied to representative works of E. M. Delafield and Angela Thirkell, as well as Jane Austen's *Pride and Prejudice*, and the recurrence reflects, as nothing else can, not only the verisimilitude of the characters, but also the general serious critical reception of the comedy of manners novels between the early 1920s and the early 1940s. The first appearance of this criticism is in 1925, in J. B. Priestley's assessment of Longbourn's reception of Mr. Collins: that Mr. Bennet anticipates Mr. Collins's silliness and relishes it upon his arrival, but his appreciation does not extend to suffering Mr. Collins in his library. Mr. Bennet, "like us, could have read about Mr. Collins forever, but having to meet him in the flesh and listen to his unexpurgated talk, he quickly tired, as we should have done."[7]

In 1930 the literary critic Louis Kronenberger makes a similar comment about E. M. Delafield's *The Diary of a Provincial Lady*: "She has made us experience vicariously with a great deal of relish what we would not experience in the flesh for a great deal of money."[8]

The last of these judgments appeared in 1942, in a review of Angela Thirkell's wartime novel *Marling Hall*: "(Thirkell's) great talent, like that of E. F. Benson in the exquisite Lucia series, is . . . for delineating people whom one would walk miles to avoid in real life, but who have a wonderful nuisance value in mere fiction."[9] These comments can be regarded as expressions of a community of interest, a familiarity with humor, and a readiness to take a character seriously over a particular period that went back to the Edwardians, from about the 1880s to 1914.

Nevertheless, there were others who found such humor frivolous and unworthy. In 1894, when *The Dolly Dialogues* was published, a slight but wildly popular[10] comedy of manners novel by Anthony Hope, the reviewer termed its hero "an elderly young man . . . too silly to think about serious things" and belittled its humor: "These conversations do not make a substantial book or an elevating one, or one that would have been missed if it had never been written."[11] There is an underlying, periodic bias against humor, with the authors themselves skeptical of its worth. Perhaps to guard himself against such criticism, Benson frankly stated that the Lucia novels were "not offered as examples of serious fiction" *(FE* 184), and 45 years later Stephen Pile acknowledges Benson's feelings: "Like many humourous writers, E. F. Benson agonized about not writing some great, unreadably serious work."[12] This concern is echoed in Jane Austen's half-mocking comment to her sister, Cassandra, that "(*Pride and Prejudice*) is rather too light, and bright, and sparkling; it wants shade; it wants to be stretched out with a long chapter of sense . . . ." (*L* 77 299-300), as well as in a feeling statement by E. M. Delafield that the harder-won artistry of her novels that were *not* the Provincial Lady Diaries "remained comparatively unhonoured and unsung."[13]

Benson's anxious denial, reflecting his failure to understand the value of his creations, was effectively dismissed by more objective and appreciative critics of his time, as stated in his obituary and, later, in the authoritative *Twentieth Century Literary Criticism*: "Benson had the enviable gift of an effortless, natural style" and "satiric irony" in the "emotional contours of Lucia and the malice of Miss Mapp,"[14] and Lucia is "one of the most memorable comic creatures in English fiction."[15] Memories of Benson by his contemporaries that were later collected and published include one comment that "the Thirties were a serious time and (the Lucia novels) were probably considered too trivial,"[16] although this is contradicted by the assertion of another friend that they "were a cult up to and even during the Second World War."[17] Such comments would seem to relegate comedy to the status of the novel mocked by John Thorpe and defended ironically by

Jane Austen's narrative voice in *Northanger Abbey*:

> . . . slighting the performances which have only genius, wit, and taste to recommend them . . . only a novel . . . (containing) the most thorough knowledge of human nature,the happiest delineation of its varieties, the liveliest effusions of wit and humour are conveyed to the world in the best chosen language. (*NA* 37)

What happened to the Jane Austen tradition and to its twentieth-century authors between the early 1940s and the late 1970s?   Stephen Pyle conjectures that Benson's "corrosive, comic voice" was one of the reasons the Lucia novels were lost sight of after his death in 1939:

> The cynicism of the 1920s and 1930s was replaced by a wholesome "we're all in it together" spirit so necessary in times of war and after. In the 1940s and 1950s we could not face Benson's relentless mockery . . . of the English race and way of life . . . .   In the 1960s and 1970s we were flower power idealists and the tiniest bit socialist . . . .   We could not face any writer so unforgiving as Benson until the arrival of novelists . . . who pride themselves on having no illusions; the time is right for a serious Benson revival.[18]

In terms of social history, Pyle's reasoning about Benson's eclipse, at least to the extent of the Lucia novels' being out of print for almost 40 years, may have been accurate, but *cynicism*, *relentless mockery*, *unforgiving*, and *corrosive* are at the far end of the critical spectrum from writer and critic V. S. Pritchett's view of Benson.   In 1980 he associated Benson's subject and style of high comedy with the Edwardians: "Whether they are writing about manners high, middling, or low, the light novelists have a common quality: they are accomplished, they are even elegant."[19]   Pritchett's interpretation reflects a more comprehensive view.

In 1977, when the six Lucia novels were reissued as *Make Way for Lucia,* humor appears to have become respectable again, with some reviews that are both more lighthearted and more serious about comedy.   Writer Nancy Mitford, a Lucia aficionado, says that the novels remain "fresh as paint."[20]   In another review Auberon Waugh comments, "Without this reissue I might have gone to my grave without ever knowing about Lucia or

Miss Mapp. It is not a risk anyone should take lightly." He calls Lucia "a superbly ridiculous woman" and describes Benson's comedy "as exquisite, in its way, as anything in English humorous literature."[21] As a measure of the immediate popular reception of the novels, paperback reprints followed, as well as a four-part television series, *Mapp and Lucia*, produced by the BBC in 1986. Then, in the spirit of those who have had the audacity to "complete" the Jane Austen fragments, *The Watsons* and *Sanditon*, a new Lucia adventure appeared, based on Benson's characters and called *Lucia in Wartime*, by Tom Holt.

"There is the Italian with which Lucia and Georgie pepper their conversation. . . . On at least two occasions an Italian turns up and then we learn that Lucia and Georgino mio don't really know the language at all. . . ." [22]

Apart from the more problematic societal question of the timeliness of humor, what has to be faced with comedy of manners novels is the criticism of both lack of plot and character development. The novels of Benson have been subjected to this criticism, as indeed were those of Jane Austen, at least until the twentieth century. But Benson's extravagant use of language—the whimsy, the incongruity, the exaggerations, and the unexpected analogies with which he makes fun of Tilling's farcical heroines—sets an exciting stage for the enclosed little worlds of Riseholme and Tilling. Benson makes an operatic reference: Tilling at different moments is likened to the second act of *Die Meistersinger* (*TWL* 112) and to the feuding of the Montagues and the Capulets (*TWL* 114). Elizabeth Bennet's facetious remark to her sister Jane that "it would be the death of half the good people in Meryton, to attempt to place (Mr. Darcy) in an amiable light" (*P&P* 226), including, as it does, the elopement and the call to action that followed it, which strongly involved the interest of the community, suggests a parallel for this dramatic crowd scene.

In addition, the characters are accompanied by *leitmotifs*. Lucia has "birdlike" eyes and speech: "Sometimes (Georgie) wished he had a piece of green baize to throw over her as over a canary, when it will not stop singing. ('Foljambe, fetch Mrs. Lucas's baize,' he thought to himself)" (*TWL* 108). Miss Mapp's *motif* is battle language: "strategic campaign" and "opening move" (*MM* 181) signal her personality, followed by "begin(s) to lash her tail," to the tune of "revenge," "smoking altar," "torture," "counterstroke," "battle," and "corpses," among others (*MM* 92). This adversarial analogy is carried through, and turned upon her, when she is revealed as hoarding food in the cupboard in the garden room:

> (There) came a noise of rattling, bumping and clattering. Something soft and heavy thumped onto the floor, and a cloud of floury dust arose. A bottle of Bovril embedded itself quietly there without damage, and a tin of Bath Oliver biscuits beat a fierce tattoo on one of the corned beef. Innumerable dried apricots from the burst package flew about like shrapnel, and tapped at the tins. (*MM* 118)

When describing this ludicrous situation from the viewpoint of the person about to expose her, Benson turns to incongruously dignified but expressive language: "With a stroke of intuition, too sure to be called a guess, Diva was aware that she had correctly inferred the storage of this nefarious hoard. It only remained to verify her conclusion, and, if possible, expose it with every circumstance of public infamy" (94). Diva does not have the flair for calumny and self-aggrandizement that Miss Mapp has, but she is human as well as fair-minded; the language relating to her in this instance, therefore, is both triumphant and even-handed.

Neither Benson nor Jane Austen is a stranger to the play on words. Benson's irresistibly vicious *bon mots*, "hoardings of dead oxen" (*MM* 93) and "the yield of a thousand condensed Swiss cows" (*MM* 113), characterize Miss Mapp's trove of food. He creates a participle, "Foljambizing," to describe the work of Georgie's newly married parlormaid, who keeps her maiden name during the day because "her life's work was Foljambizing to Georgie" (*TWL* 16). These can be linked to the Jane Austen tradition; for example, Mr. Bennet's announcement that the Collinses are expecting an "olive branch" mocks in one stroke the presumption of Mr. Collins in his efforts as peacemaker.

"Voluptuous teas were the rule" (MM 27).

Because in Tilling there is so little in the way of love interest to be talked about on High Street, in contrast with the matrimonial prospects of Jane Austen's heroines, Benson has substituted food and appearance as engrossing topics. Food has always been an integral element of the comedy of manners because mealtimes—breakfast, lunch, tea, and dinner—become rituals for the family and, on more formal social occasions, include guests. In recent years the roles of food in literature, including its symbolism, have been the subject of critical scholarship. In Tilling, although few dinners are given, except by Lucia, rigid custom reminiscent of Elizabeth Gaskell's *Cranford* several generations earlier dictates the appropriate refreshments to be offered at bridge and tea: "It was considered vulgar to give anything expensive in the way of eatable or drinkable, at the evening entertainments . . . money-spending was always 'vulgar and ostentatious'" (*Cranford* 5). In Cranford, this attitude is called "elegant economy." All the single ladies are hospitable, but those in more straitened circumstances do not have to compete with the one or two who are better off. When the opportunity arises, however, as it does with Miss Betty Barker's "abundantly loaded" tea-tray, the good Amazons might whisper to each other that Miss Barker, a former ladies'-maid, can not be expected to know better, yet they take full advantage of what is offered. Isabel Poppit, a relative newcomer to Tilling, makes the same social error by presenting "a buffet vulgarly heaped . . . so vulgar and opulent that with one accord everyone set to work in earnest, in order that the garden should present a less gross and greedy appearance" (*MM* 35).

Jane Austen's Mrs. Norris is the forerunner of the Cranford and Tilling critics of plenty. She makes it her business to find out the habits of the new occupants of Mansfield Parsonage:

> The Dr. was very fond of eating and would have a good dinner every day; and Mrs. Grant, instead of contriving to gratify him at little expense, gave her cook as high wages as they did at Mansfield Park. . . . Mrs. Norris could not speak with any temper of such grievances, nor of the quantity of butter and eggs that were regularly consumed in the house. 'Nobody loved plenty and hospitality more than herself—nobody more hated pitiful doings. . . . Her storeroom she thought might have been good enough for Mrs. Grant to go into.' (*MP* 31)

Such hypocrisy is indispensable to the comedy of manners.

Besides the matter of custom regarding food, and in the comedy of manners any deviation from the prevailing norm is derided, competition and envy about food result in the most dramatic adventure in the annals of Tilling. The rituals connected with food become an arena of domestic power struggle. It is the custom there for the hostess, if asked, to share her recipe for a particular culinary success; whether measurements of ingredients are recorded absolutely accurately is a separate consideration. Lucia does not respond to Miss Mapp's requests for the secret of "Lobster à la Riseholme," even thwarting efforts to bribe the cook. Undaunted, Miss Mapp seizes the moment when Lucia's house is deserted on Christmas Eve to enter the kitchen surreptitiously, find and copy the coveted recipe and, just as Lucia returns, replace the cookbook on the shelf. Accusations and recriminations have to be put aside because the flood waters, which have been rising all day, sweep in, and together they are carried out to sea on the overturned kitchen table. Years later, Benson's friend Sir Steven Runciman considers Benson's sending Lucia and Miss Mapp out to sea on Lucia's overturned kitchen table an inspiration: "it is masterly, and lifts the novel out of the social comedy on to a wider horizon of fantastic and surrealistic humour."[26]

Appearance is not just another element in the comedy of manners; it is an overriding concern. Jane Austen has Elinor Dashwood picture Lucy Ferrars as "the active, contriving manager, uniting at once a desire of smart appearance, with the utmost frugality, and ashamed to be suspected of half her economical practices" (*S&S* 357). Mrs. Norris, in charge of the green baize curtain for the theatricals at Mansfield Park, takes pride in contriving to make just as good a show with less than the number of curtain rings ordered (*MP* 141). Lucy's smart appearance is intended to cover her inferiority of education and lack of culture; Mrs. Norris is officious in her fancied indispensableness and in her delighted superiority in saving the absent Sir Thomas insignificant amounts of money, not noticing the larger family concerns and her complete inadequacy in understanding.

In a different, more contemporary, aspect of appearance, Emma is "fancying what the observations of all those might be, who were now seeing (Frank Churchill and her) together for the first time" (*E* 212); "They were a couple worth looking at" (230). In terms of recent criticism, by Emma's "forming a thousand amusing schemes for the progress and close of their attachment, fancying interesting dialogues, and inventing elegant letters . . . " and conclusions for this romance (264), she is "fictionizing" herself,[24] critic Patricia Spacks suggests.

In Lucia Lucas, Benson has brought the art of appearance to its highest level. When we first meet her, Lucia has arrived home in Riseholme from London and has sent home the cab with her luggage but without her. She knows that her husband will simply conclude that she has walked, but the people of Riseholme will be baffled. Benson's authorial voice informs the reader that "these guesses at what other people would think when they saw it arrive without her sprang from the dramatic element that formed so large a part of her mentality" (*QL* 12, 13). What other people think and how she might appear—wants to appear—to them is what Lucia thrives on. She even has a musical signature: she plays, with a rapt, faraway, slow-movement look put on for the occasion, the first movement of the "Moonlight Sonata" because it is slower and makes her seem a more substantial pianist than she is. When the year of absolute mourning for her husband is almost up and her friend Daisy telephones to consult about the forthcoming Riseholme fete, Lucia debates "whether she would be found at the piano, playing the funeral march from Beethoven's 'Sonata in A flat,' which she now knew by heart, or be sitting out in Perdita's garden, reading Peppino's (her husband's) poems" (*M&L* 4).

There is less farce but just as much insincerity in appearances in Jane Austen's bringing together Lucy Steele, who is secretly engaged to Edward Ferrars, and Elinor Dashwood, who as Lucy's unwilling confidante has been taken by surprise because she believes that Edward is sincerely attracted to *her.* "The two fair rivals were thus seated side by side at the same table, and with the utmost harmony engaged in forwarding the same work" (*S&S* 145), the "little sharp eyes" of Lucy full of meaning, and "Elinor . . . careful in guarding her countenance from every expression that could give her words a suspicious tendency" (146, 7).

After every pitched battle between them, Lucia and Miss Mapp walk in to dinner smiling and with arms wreathed around each other's waist. Elinor and Lucy are duelling over love; but Lucia and Miss Mapp are duelling over power, and it is a seesaw match, because the circle—Tilling—is still the focus. The same one cannot always dominate. In a similar vein, but one that is both more serious and more far-reaching, Emma and Mrs. Elton have no way of escaping each other: Mrs. Elton, as the wife of the minister, is second only to Mrs. Weston in the rigid social hierarchy of the village, and Emma, of course, is always first. But for Mr. Knightley's influence, Highbury might easily see more of the thinly papered-over fundamental "state of warfare" (*E* 282) between the two young women. Insincerity is emphatically the cornerstone of these relationships; at the same time, these women are creating a drama to enliven their existences, for in the comedy of manners the village puts particular constraints upon their actions and words. Emma Woodhouse especially has little opportunity for further self-realization in Highbury. Lucia realizes that there is nothing and no one to challenge her in Riseholme any longer, so she begins all over in Tilling as a summer renter and eventually secures for herself the "big house" of Mallards and the office of Mayor of Tilling.

"(Olga Braceley) is the only ideal figure in the book, as poor Georgie Pillson is the only other good-natured one." [25]

The criticism of insufficient character development in the comedy of manners novels is no longer seen as true for Jane Austen's novels. In recent critical thinking, her heroines Elizabeth Bennet and Emma Woodhouse have a moment of epiphany that makes them mature enough for the ideal marriage. Benson's Lucia never advances in self-knowledge. *Mastery of character,* however, is where the writers of the comedy of manners shine. Jane Austen created the irrepressible Mr. Collins, whose absurdities have always been appreciated by readers, but J. B. Priestley's imaginative description of him as ". . . entering Fairyland" strikes a response in students and lovers of her novels. She is also the creator of that general favorite, Mr. Woodhouse, and of garrulous Miss Bates (*E*). Miss Bates might be thought of but is not treated by her community as tiresome, and although she was regarded by earlier readers as inconsequential, she has a dramatic purpose limited to the secret engagement between Jane Fairfax and Frank Churchill. She reveals, artlessly and, at times, ironically because Emma does not pay any attention to what she has to say, Frank's frequent, domesticated presence at the Bateses' apartments and his assiduous care of aunt and niece at the ball at the Crown.

Benson is regarded by critics as a worthy bearer of the torch passed along by the creator of Mr. Collins and Miss Bates: Lucia is considered a "memorable comic character." Why did such on-stage, public people as Noel Coward and Gertrude Lawrence, elegant actors of a bygone generation, cherish her? Benson's two small towns, Riseholme and Tilling, "where almost everybody wanted to be somebody,"[26] are little worlds, stages for the productions of which Lucia claims all the credits, managing, producing, doing the star turn, and always acting a part. She is forever conscious of appearance in the role she is playing. She chooses clothes immediately identifying her as the leader of the yoga and meditation group, and leader of the physical fitness group, for she immediately volunteers to teach all of Riseholme or Tilling anything the minute she has mastered it herself; it is only fair to add that she is a quick study. But she is unwilling to exploit her official status by wearing her mayoral robes for the opening of Diva's tea room.

Lucia never holds grudges or replays old bridge hands, as does Miss Mapp. She is a maker of grand gestures; when they backfire, she moves on to something fresh. She is the first to ride a bicycle, practising in private, of course, and the first to invest in the stock market. She capitalizes on Georgie's ideas, telling him how clever she was to produce, at the right moment, the letter in Italian he had arranged to be written for her, getting them both out of a tight spot; but when Miss Mapp puts the picture Georgie has painted for her in the bargain tray at her rummage sale, Lucia annihilates her.

From a modern point of view, Benson's treatment of Georgie Pillson makes him an intriguing character in the novels. Georgie and Lucia affect the codes of baby talk or strictly limited Italian, and he wears little capes, dyes his hair to appear young, polishes his bibelots, and works *petit-point* shepherdesses. Benson gives him no male companion, young or old, nor does he refer to any sexual preference, except for Georgie's fear of Lucia's expectations of him. His role as foil for Lucia, first as devoted admirer and then husband, contributes to the irony that makes him old-maidish and her intrepid.

"She always called him 'Padre,' and had never actually caught him looking over his adversaries' (bridge) hands" (*MM* 31).

Benson includes a resident clergyman among the three or four families in Tilling. The Padre has idiosyncrasies, but they are completely different from those of Jane Austen's clergymen. A major difference is that the Padre is not a contender for the hand of the heroine and is therefore more peripheral than pivotal in the village group. A second, and equally major, difference is in theological appropriateness. Jane Austen's Edmund Bertram is serious about his duties as pastor at Thornton Lacey, his living, and as moral role model for his flock, while his friend Henry Crawford speaks of the pleasures of hearing and even preaching an eloquent sermon, but "(preaching) would not do for a constancy" (*MP* 341). The Padre's particular *motif* is Scotch or Irish or earlier dialects, or a confusing mixture of all three, and he may take a look at his opponent's bridge hand, but he is not a sycophant, as Mr. Collins is. More important, his perorations from the pulpit, although criticized for their content or grammar or style by Miss Mapp, are very much to the point of what is going on in Tilling. This well-intentioned man of the cloth puts himself in the line of fire by trying to forestall a duel between Major Flint and Captain Puffin that never occurs. Although the situation is farcical, it is important that his flock firmly believes it is his duty to intervene. The humor Benson directs at him is, therefore, more affectionate and less satirical.

Those slums ought to be swept away altogether, and new houses built tutto presto (TWL 103).

Edmund Bertram's status as a younger son, with a lesser income, and Henry's position as a wealthy landowner with a dilettante's view of the parish priest's role, brings us to the significance of the characters' economic circumstances in the comedy of manners. It is not that money and what it can buy are not frequently alluded to by Lucia's circle, but those circumstances have more to do with social status and attitude than with the courtesy and concerns of landed aristocracy as portrayed in the Jane Austen novels. When Georgie tells Lucia that it is "very generous" of her to have had the hillside approach to Tilling beautified with almond trees and its dilapidated steps put in good order, and to have had a number of dramatic new stops added to the church organ, she replies, "No, dear; simple duty"; that she has made 8000 pounds on the Stock Exchange and wants to benefit Tilling (*TWL* 345). These ploys, however, are more political than philanthropic: Lucia is purchasing goodwill as benefactress of Tilling, her eye not only on the presidency of the Tilling cricket society but also on higher things—the mayoralty, as it turns out.

Benson's characters exhibit little class consciousness of the kind associated with certain characters of Jane Austen's, such as Mr. Knightley's *noblesse oblige* in sending his carriage to convey Miss Bates and Jane Fairfax to the Coles' on a cold evening, but done with a lack of ostentation (*E* 223). When Lucia sends her car to Tilling to bring her bridge guests to Grebe, some quarter-mile out of town, she does so less with the intent of being considered thoughtful than as a maneuver to get them there in the face of Elizabeth Mapp's competing invitation. Lucia has learned from experience: one rainy evening, when she is still a summer renter at Mallards and does *not* offer her car for the musical evening, the next morning her guests are rebellious.

Another comparison reinforces this difference in attitude. When Mr. Knightley gives his remaining store of apples to the Bateses, Miss Bates tells him that Jane is "shocked"; that is, she is angry at forever being put in this position. Elizabeth Mapp, however, can afford to return Lucia's largess of tomatoes and, after a resounding, but temporary, defeat at her hands, Miss Mapp says that she cannot go on being grateful for Lucia's generosity. This defiance/accommodation scenario provides the framework of comedy in the novels, as Tilling thrives on the excitement of watching one of its contenders for leadership bite the hand that feeds her.

Emma, Jane Austen's heroine of whom she wrote "no one but myself will much like,"[29] is "handsome, clever, and rich" (*E* 5), and class conscious. When Mr. Knightley taxes her with not being the friend to Jane Fairfax that she should be, Emma's excuse is "the horror of being in danger of falling in with the second rate and third rate of Highbury" at the Bateses' (155). When Emma hears of the Coles' projected dinner party, who she allows are "very respectable in their way" (207), that is, they are members of the rising middle class, she "hardly supposes" that "they would presume to invite . . . the regular and best families . . . neither Donwell, Hartfield, nor Randalls" (207). Nonetheless, she allows herself to be persuaded to accept the Colesu' invitation because she wants to be where her friends are. This class attitude is still exhibited in Tilling, for when it comes to the absolute necessity of Miss Mapp's finding out what has happened to Captain Puffin on Christmas Eve, she approaches the voluble group on High Street, the accepted meeting place even on a holiday, and "Though Mrs. Brace (the doctor's wife) was not, strictly speaking, 'in society,' Miss Mapp waived all social distinctions and pressed her hand with a mournful smile" (*MM* 292).

Tilling, and Riseholme before it, are a way of life, a collective reaction, opinion, judgment: "As for Riseholme . . . but it was better not to think how she (Lucia) stood with regard to Riseholme" (*LL*152); "It must be lived down, and if dear old Riseholme was offended with her, Riseholme must be propitiated" (*LL*160). Such collective references acknowledge what is quite clear: that the community, meaning public opinion, although only that of the three or four families, must be taken into account by both Lucia and Elizabeth Mapp. Miss Mapp arrives at a fairly accurate reading of the shifts in public opinion about her outrageous coups by using the transparent Diva as the barometer of the Tilling climate. By "tapping" her, Miss Mapp can retract (rarely), prevaricate (frequently), brazen through (brilliantly) or, as she says, "scriggle" out of the predicament.

"Cook had returned in a state of high indignation, which possibly she had expressed by saturating Lucia's soup with pepper, and putting so much mustard into her devilled chicken that it might have been used as a plaster for the parlormaid" (TFL 301).

Where Benson makes a contribution to the comedy of manners is in introducing the servants, having them interact more with the major characters, perhaps showing himself to be more aware of that class than Jane Austen is. One of his long-time friends affirms this awareness: Benson "would have known the minutiae of behaviour lower down the social scale" from his "intense interest in what was going on, both from his own keen observation, and what he learned from gossip."[27] The inclusion of the servants has been glowingly described by Queenie Leavis in her characterization of English novelists: "They took as their province a society revealed from top to bottom and all characters shown as mutually dependent and as affected by the rest, and all equally seen with respect and compassion."[28] Although Jane Austen has been criticized for not having the servants perform a more significant role, they do appear more in *Mansfield Park* than in her earlier novels. They are useful in showing the change in Fanny Price's status and her importance in the household, for we see them mostly in conjunction with Fanny and Mrs. Norris. Baddeley, the butler, in particular, is part of some significant moments. For Fanny's first ball he prepares a "noble" fire, which Mrs. Norris is soon occupied in disarranging. He is important to Fanny in bearing a message summoning her to Sir Thomas's room, to hear Mr. Crawford's proposal, as it turns out, interjecting a note of humor when he refutes Mrs. Norris's immediate assumption that the message is for *her*. "But Baddeley was stout . . . . And there was a half smile with the words which meant, 'I do not think *you* would answer the purpose at all" (325). On another evening, when Fanny is importuned by Mr. Crawford, ironically it is not Fanny's cousin Edmund, her usual protector, and the only one who is aware of her feelings about

Crawford, who rescues her, but Baddeley—and with the ceremony of after-dinner tea:

> the sound of approaching relief, the very sounds which she had been long watching for, and long thinking strangely delayed. The solemn procession, headed by Baddeley, of tea-board, urn, and cake-bearers made its appearance and delivered her from a grievous imprisonment of body and mind. Mr. Crawford was obliged to move. She was at liberty, she was busy, she was protected. (344)

The domestic comedy of manners, after all, revolves around the conventions of meal times.

Then there is Chapman, eternally frozen in Lady Bertram's memory, and ours, as having been sent, although dispatched too late, to help Fanny dress for her first ball. Without a doubt Lady Bertram, ordinarily passive to a fault, has become animated with her plan and dismisses Chapman before she otherwise might, saying, "That is perfectly splendid, and now. . . ."

Mrs. Poppit, maligned as *nouveau riche* by Tilling, led by Miss Mapp, although soon given the essential Faraglione old family cachet by Mr. Wyse, is still somewhat in awe of Boon, her butler, as is Miss Mapp, her usual derider: "Boon opened the door to her three staccato little knocks, and sulkily consulted his list . . . . 'And may I put my sketching things down here, please, Boon,' said Miss Mapp ingratiatingly" (*MM* 34). Her courtesy is reminiscent of the Cranford ladies' little pleasantries to propitiate Mrs. Jamison's Mr. Mulliner, "an object of great awe to all of us. . . . Miss Pole ventured on a small joke as we went upstairs, intended, though addressed to us, to offer Mr. Mulliner some slight amusement" (*Cranford* 119). Also in *Cranford* Mary Smith is unwilling to thwart Miss Matty Jenkyns's loyal servant Martha in the latter's sudden wedding plans and her special pudding lion for dinner to show her resourceful sympathy for her impoverished and bewildered mistress.[29]

Benson makes much more of the employers' dependence on their servants. An extreme example is Georgie Pilson's symbiotic relationship with his faithful Foljambe. If that peerless parlourmaid is not happy with him, tepid bath water and fluff on his clothes result. Her "singing in a high buzzing voice . . . a rancid noise" (*M&L* 160) tells him that she is contented with her lot, because his first concern in making the move from Riseholme to Tilling and renting delightful Mallards Cottage is whether Foljambe will be happy there. When he finds out that she wants to marry Cadman, Lucia's chauffeur, Georgie says, "She's been with me fifteen years, and now she breaks up my home like that" (88), very much as though he were talking about a wife or mistress rather than a parlormaid. Upon Lucia's suggesting that Cadman would like her to be at home at night, "Horrible to think of," Georgie says. "I wonder what she can see in him" (90), which in a master/servant relationship sounds inappropriately personal. He takes advantage of their relationship by saying, "Or would it be better to be very cold and preoccupied and not talk to her at all? She'd hate that, and then, when I ask her after some days whether she'll stop on with me, she might promise anything to see me less unhappy again" (89). Finally, when he is apprehensive about being pursued by Duchess Poppy, and Lucia suggests that he sleep in her room for one night, they having been married for some time, he refuses: "Oh, I don't think either of us would like that," and "Foljambe would think it so odd" (*TFL* 290).

Benson arranges for Foljambe to marry Cadman and still take care of Georgie during the day. He also brings together in matrimony Elizabeth Mapp and Major Flint, however unlikely the union, because this is a society in which servants are so important that someone would go to unexpected lengths to obtain them. This couple, therefore, epitomizes W. H. Auden's reaction to what he considers Jane Austen's propensity for having her heroines find and marry a man of substance:

> It makes me most uncomfortable to see
> An English spinster of the middle class
> Describe the amorous effects of 'brass',
> Reveal so frankly and with such sobriety

The economic basis of society.[30]

In Tilling, the *economic basis of society*, including the dependence on servants, is an undeniable impetus to matrimony. Major Flint is retired, has an Army pension, and lives relatively modestly, although he figures in the constant tea and bridge hospitality of the single women and married couples. He does keep two servants, who make all the difference when it comes to domestic comfort for their master. For years Miss Mapp has been trying to inveigle him into marrying her, even though he has only that Army pension, and she is a "woman of substance, in every sense of the word" (*TWL* 19). He has become discredited, however, because he moves into Mallards, his legacy from her, while she and Lucia are still out on the cod banks, the denouement of their fantastic adventure upon the upturned kitchen table. In addition, he is humiliated by being thrown out of the house by Miss Mapp upon her return, his false teeth left on the doorstep, and he is impoverished, in part by paying the wages of her servants. His most misguided move has been to let his own servants go, upon establishing himself at Mallards. What Benson does not say, although he talks around it, is that without any servants—and none are immediately available— to cook his food or provide order and comfort at home, it has come to the point that if Major Benjy, as Miss Mapp coyly calls him, wants any status or comfort in Tilling, he has no economic or social recourse but to marry her. His capitulation to her comes in a note: "Your forgiveness, should you be so gracious as to extend it to me, will much mitigate my present situation" (*M&L* 273). It is economic reality as well as social necessity; and "There was no reason for (in fact, every reason against) a long engagement" (279).

On the traditional level of keeping up appearances, the servants in the novel of manners are supposed to be kept ignorant of any family scandal and at one remove from community intrigues and gossip. Jane Austen has Elizabeth Bennet anxiously maintain this fiction when she asks her sister Jane whether there is a servant who does not know the whole story of

Lydia's elopement. Riseholme and Tilling observe the same conventions: Lucia says, "*Tacit*, Georgino. *Les domestiches*," and "she took refuge in Italian as Grosvenor appeared" (*M&L* 59).

We happily note that Georgie's Foljambe, Daisy Quantock's de Vere, and Lucia's Grosvenor rejoice in much grander names than their respective master and mistresses.

While Benson's Lucia novels carry on the Jane Austen tradition in terms of social satire, the similarities also are a result of the lack of major structural change in British society in the one hundred and eighteen years from Jane Austen's time to World War II. This society continued to be made up of rural communities led by the gentry in the Great House and to be centered around the three or four families and the villagers. The features of the comedy of manners, strictures more important than law, remain unchanged: the choreography of the dinner parties follows the classic steps; and the shopping expeditions of Emma and Harriet to the center of Highbury continue through the nineteenth century in those of Miss Matty Jenkyns and the narrator of *Cranford,* to the daily drama of the High Street in Tilling.

Nevertheless, it is the nature of individual creativity, however strong Benson's affinity for Jane Austen, that his novels cannot help being his own; and it is a tribute to Benson's writing in the Jane Austen tradition of the comedy of manners that critics again consider his novels "fresh as paint" and "comic masterpieces." Continuing tradition, Benson has created a heroine, Emmeline "Lucia" Lucas, who, like Mr. Collins, is larger than life and has an existence beyond the novels.

2

E. M. Delafield

"Speak of this to Robert, who returns no answer . . . .
This suggests Query: Does Robert, perhaps, take in what
I say even when he makes no reply?" (DPL 4).

In 1813, when Jane Austen was visiting her brother Henry in London following the publication of *Pride and Prejudice*, she was already in a fair way to being lionized. She wrote to her sister, Cassandra, "If I am a wild Beast, I cannot help it. It is not my own fault" (*L* 80 311). Henry apparently found it irresistible to reveal her identity as the author of the novel to all his acquaintances, for the title page identified the author only as "the Author of *Sense and Sensibility*." But she did not remain in London, and there is no evidence that she regretted not being part of the literary scene there. Instead, she continued this most productive and rewarding period of her life in the family atmosphere of Chawton, with both *Mansfield Park* and *Emma* published and *Persuasion* completed before she died in 1817.

Approximately one hundred fifteen years later, E. M. Delafield was part of a literary circle in London. She did not have to depend on her father, and then a brother, as Jane Austen did, to make arrangements for her novels to be published. Her Provincial Lady Diaries chronicle, for the first time, the day-to-day life of a contemporary woman who was at once wife, mother, and writer, and who eventually acquired a tiny flat in London in which to write—when her children were back at school. This woman was the Provincial Lady, and because she, too, wrote, is Delafield's persona, author-as-writer. "EMD," as Delafield signed those diary entries, was one of a fine crop of strong women writers flourishing in the 1920s and 1930s who frequently have been neglected, for after World War II the literary climate for their standing as writers and independent women changed. During those two decades between the two world wars, however, the domestic arrangements of most of these women, that is, being married and having children, as well as writing, meant, just as it did for Jane Austen, that writing was one of their many tasks.

Women today, not only feminists, but scholars, writers, and readers, are very much interested in how women lived in the past and how those lives are narrated by women who wrote. The works of women are being explored for how they felt about themselves and what the conditions of their lives were, women like Delafield, whose writing has gone through the stages of popularity, eclipse, rediscovery, and now, some measure of recognition.

To help answer the question, Why did women write? Elaine Showalter, in "reinterpreting the works of women writers and documenting their lives and careers,"[1] divides the time between Jane Austen and E. M. Delafield, and later, into four overlapping periods: first, the *female literary tradition*, meaning that women wrote in the tradition established by men, a pertinent example being Jane Austen's admiration for Samuel Johnson's style, although not to the extent of imitating it. Hard upon this came the *feminine* novelists, including both Charlotte Brontë and George Eliot, who described the lives of ordinary women. This was followed by an intensely *feminist* period, from 1880 to 1920, which included experimental forms of literature, notably those of Virginia Woolf, with the subject matter frequently a "protest against those (feminine) standards and values, and advocacy of minority rights and values."[2] From about 1920 to the present, a *female aesthetic* of self-discovery developed, with a new self-awareness from 1960 onwards.

Most important in providing a rationale for Delafield's emergence as a comedy-of-manners writer in the Jane Austen tradition is Showalter's statement that women writers in the 1930s "attacked the refinement, incorporality, and inaction" of Woolf's novels; they "rejected the experimentation of modernism"; they "wanted to lead imaginative lives."[3] Delafield was an established novelist and a member of the board of *Time and Tide*, a feminist-oriented literary weekly founded in 1920, at the time she began the weekly series of topical sketches called "Diary of a Provincial Lady." The first installment appeared on December 6, 1929, and the following year the sketches were published in book form, with the same title. Delafield later said that she had been asked by the editor of *Time and Tide*, Lady Rhondda, to write a "new light series" for the paper, and "with the Micawber-like conviction that something would turn up. . . I agreed to do so."[4]

Although the diary, or journal, was an experimental form for Delafield and for the comedy of manners, the journal form was hardly a new one in 1929. Pepys, Boswell, Parson Woodforde, and Kilvert kept diaries that have contributed not only to our pleasure but also to our knowledge of their times: they are an almost unsurpassable source of social history. Delafield describes her intentions in terms that help reveal her creative impulse:

> The idea had come into my mind of writing, in the first person singular, a perfectly straightforward account of the many disconcerting facets presented by everyday life to the average woman . . . . I wrote the instalments almost as they appeared, keeping just ahead of publication. This was partly to ensure that any comments on public affairs would be reasonably up-to-date.[5]

The Diary of a Provincial Lady is also similar to the popular serialized novels of the nineteenth century that were written and released chapter by chapter or, rather, episode by episode, in weekly and monthly installments. Elizabeth Gaskell's *Cranford* was one of these, as were Dickens's and Thackeray's novels. The Provincial Lady Diaries are also in the tradition of the epistolary novel, the form in which both *Sense and Sensibility* and *Pride and Prejudice* had their origins; nevertheless, the Diaries began as personal essays discussing current topics of interest, and, therefore, Delafield's writings of the 1930s are as fresh now as they were then, illustrating and recapturing that era. This focus applies to her depiction of life in the English countryside—those "three or four families in a country village"—in 1930 (*Diary of a Provincial Lady*), to the London literary circle of that time (*The Provincial Lady in London*) (1932), and also to early wartime (1939–1940) England (*The Provincial Lady in Wartime*), in perhaps the most topical of the diaries.

Showalter's time line connects Jane Austen and Delafield in an overall picture, for the essential reason that "a special female self-awareness emerges through literature in every period,"[6] but it has been the unusual woman who has tried to break out of her traditionally imposed, and stereotypical, womanly quietness, acquiescence, and compliance, and to define herself in her own terms, not as an adjunct to her father, husband, or son. Delafield is one woman who not only manages to do so, but also goes on to record her experiences, using a form of writing different from her previous novels.   This creative aspect of a woman's life has characteristically been downplayed or even denied existence. After Jane Austen's death, her brother Henry Austen chose to slight her writing talent, emphasizing instead her steadfast religious faith and sterling domestic qualities. Furthermore, in the *Memoir* (1870), her nephew James Edward Austen-Leigh created the stereotypical family member character "Aunt Jane," revealing almost nothing about her as an established writer. Commentaries such as these influenced some readers' perception of her as an author. She was regarded as a popular novelist of pleasant, but light material; only a few recognized what more recent criticism has put forward as an underlying didacticism.

Significantly, Jane Austen continued to write, though frequently a surrogate mother to her brother Edward's eleven children after his wife died, whether at his Great House in Chawton or at his house in Alton, which he made available for her and her sister, Cassandra, and their mother. The Alton house is the setting for the story that has been passed down of the door that creaked when opened, giving her, seated at her writing, warning that one of the children or a servant was approaching. As for what has been called "the business of marrying and mothering," the first of which was the central consideration for all of Jane Austen's heroines, and the second equally central for the Provincial Lady and her creator, critic Lloyd W. Brown suggests that for Jane Austen in those traditional times, "the marriage of an Austen heroine signifies the achievement of a self-sufficient and mature individualism . . . it underscores the full equality on which the relationship is now based, and which critics are now seeing as Jane Austen's essential feminism."[7] His comment represents a complete reversal in critics' perception of a writer who for years was considered a traditionalist in her views on the role of women.

Later novelists followed in Jane Austen's footsteps in attempting to break the stereotypical pattern of women's lives. E. M. Delafield was one of these women. Louis Kronenberger recognized this when he identified one important aspect of the Diaries in his review of *The Provincial Lady in London* (1932):

> The Provincial Lady's earning power and the recognition she receives in more exalted places than Little Podington . . . lead her to assert herself at times, and the tactful and devoted wife emerges . . . as a personality in her own right.[8]

Critic Margaret Lawrence described Delafield's *The Diary of a Provincial Lady*, the first of five Diaries, as "possibly the first time a woman ever set down the doings of her day-to-day life in all their simplicity and attached to them her own tentatively philosophical conclusions" and noted that Delafield "set the reading English world smiling about the funny slant of an ordinary woman's existence."[9] This is a meaningful statement, as wit, humor, and satire on their lives or the lives of their heroines had not characterized the writing of women, with the exception of those in *Cranford*, since the novels of Jane Austen.

"(Query: Why should display of duplicity in others wear more serious aspect than similar lapse in oneself? Answer comes there none.)" (*PLL* 95)

Kronenberger's statement about the Provincial Lady also leads to a fruitful consideration of autobiographical elements in the writing of the spinster, but often surrogate mother, Jane Austen, and the wife and mother, Delafield. Despite the Austen family's determination to keep Jane Austen from being remembered as remarkable, anecdotes about her writing from her writing nieces and extracts from her published letters reveal that personal details are incorporated in the novels, offering a window into Jane Austen's life and interests. For example, Edmund Bertram, who is not satirized as are both Mr. Collins and Mr. Elton, although for different reasons, offers a "window" into her beliefs with his own convictions about the role of the clergy.

Delafield's writing contained more easily discernible autobiographical elements. Answering the "inevitable" frequently asked question about how much, if any, of the Provincial Lady Diaries was taken from real life, she wrote: "As regards circumstances, almost entirely so. But then the circumstances of all of us who live in the country on small means, and struggle with children, servants, garden, and debts, are alike."[10] The Diaries were written during the Depression and, according to her daughter, Delafield was "pinched until the late 30s."[11] The *small means* are an underlying motif in the two earliest Diaries. The Provincial Lady begins, "Financial instability very trying" (*DPL* 23), and she periodically notes their being in funds through an inheritance and the advances on her writing or, far more usual, by pawning her great-aunt's diamond ring at the pawnbroker's in Portsmouth and retrieving it for an evening out, "just in time," or by selling her old clothes to a second-hand place that advertises "highest prices for outgrown garments." Their means being small is emphasized by the state of their overdraft. What is interesting is that there is not a division of labor over the responsibility of money: "April 13: Financial situation definitely tense, and inopportune arrival of Rates casts a gloom, but Robert points out that they are not due until May 28th, and am unreasonably relieved. *Query*: Why? *Reply* suggests, not for the first time, analogy with Mr. Micawber" (*DPL* 169). Robert's reassurance and the Micawber triumph-of-hope-over-experience analogy, and the Provincial Lady's being the one who must borrow against the overdraft, collectively show that she, not her husband, is the one who is responsible for the bills.

Straitened circumstances were reversed by the Provincial Lady's literary success. The accompanying financial reward results in a revealing dialogue:

> Robert and I spend pleasant evening discussing relative merits of Rolls Royce, electric light, and journey to the South of Spain—this last suggestion not favoured by Robert—but eventually decide to pay bills and Do Something about the Mortgage. Robert handsomely adds that I had better spend some of the money on myself, and what about a pearl necklace? I say Yes, to show that I am touched by his thoughtfulness, but do not commit myself to pearl necklace. Should like to suggest very small flat in London . . . . (*PLL* 6)

This diary entry incorporates several revealing considerations: first, her money will make a difference; second, she would like to get away from the confines of living in the country in favor of the South of Spain, which also is warmer and seen as more romantic than Devonshire; third, Robert *handsomely* (a generous term) stipulates that she spend some of the money on herself and accordingly suggests a pearl necklace, generally considered the traditionally unimaginative masculine idea of what a woman might like. She would like a very small flat, but is "quite unable to utter the words," which can only mean that she does not think that Robert is ready to entertain the idea of such independence on her part. Eventually, the confidence given by that measure of literary recognition and financial success, as well as strong feminist encouragement and support from her friend Rose, enable the Provincial Lady to decide in favor of the very small flat. The necessity for a deposit of two pounds brings in the everyday state of a woman's resources:

even between them the Provincial Lady and Rose have difficulty in mustering it, "mostly in florins." The implication is that this predicament of lack of money has held true for women through the centuries unless or until they have access to money by being able to earn it themselves.

Living in the country on small means limns Jane Austen's circumstances as well, as both her letters and fiction reflect. All of her six published novels, as well as the two fragments, *The Watsons* and *Sanditon*, and the earlier *Lady Susan*, are concerned with money and the fortunes of the young heroines and their consequent relationship to society. Consider Mrs. Bennet's frequent references to the entail on Longbourn and the two-fold significance of Mr. Collins's position as both suitor and relation upon whom the estate is entailed, in *Pride and Prejudice.* An unjust will deprives Elinor and Marianne Dashwood of enough financial substance to qualify as appropriate choices for Willoughby and Edward Ferrars, in *Sense and Sensibility.* Fanny Price's poverty makes her aunt and uncle Bertram advise her to accept the proposal of Henry Crawford, a man whom she does not love, to insure that she will be taken care of, in *Mansfield Park.* His misunderstanding of Catherine Morland's prospects makes General Tilney first court her, and encourage his son to court her, and then dismiss her precipitously from his house, in *Northanger Abbey.* Jane Fairfax's situation of dependence obliges her to be secretive about an engagement that would not be welcome to Frank Churchill's adoptive parents and may make her a reluctant recipient of Mrs. Elton's patronage, in *Emma. Persuasion* goes a level beyond the immediate relationship of the heroine to society in terms of financial substance. Anne Elliot's father and sister first turn down her eager lover as not equalling her in status, but in the end they must accept this successful naval officer's suit, because their improvidence has forced them to give up their ancestral home. These ironic situations illustrate the importance of economics as a factor in the social standing of the heroines and consideration of the appropriate partner for each of them.

It is almost impossible to look at Delafield's Provincial Lady Diaries without seeing the autobiographical elements. She not only used the flat in Doughty Street as background for the story but also acknowledged that the Provincial Lady's two children, Robin and Vicky, were "mild likenesses" of her own young children, and that while some of the Provincial Lady's friends and neighbors were "types, rather than portraits," some intimate friends— Rose, Felicity, Mary Kelway—"appeared by permission."[12]

Her unembellished account of how much of real life came into the Diaries is given a further dimension by her long-time editor, Lady Rhondda, who also reveals and illuminates Delafield's role in the comedy of manners:

> Here is EMD's real life. Robert and Robin and Vicky and the little house in Devonshire and the local Women's Institute meetings and the flat in Doughty Street to which she sometimes escaped to write, all those in fact existed. So, probably, at one time or another, did most of the people whom she meets in the pages of *The Diary of a Provincial Lady* . . . . Some of the minor characters were, I have reason to believe, drawn, or rather caricatured, directly from life without any softening whatsoever. That was the artist. That was the truth as she saw it, driving out the discretion proper to a semiautobiography. And that is why the book is so vividly alive. EMD always drew more directly from life than many writers do. She belonged essentially I have always thought to the critical rather than the creative brand of literature and her criticism expressed itself never in the ordinary way but always in that comparatively slight caricature that emphasizes and so reveals to us the oddities and queernesses of the world.[13]

Another contemporary profile of Delafield is available in the Foreword to the 1946 edition of the collected Diaries, where Kate O'Brien, through her perspective as a novelist, expands on the creation and role of Delafield's persona by showing another side of her personality. She colors and augments Delafield's own account of drawing on personal experiences and, later, for *A Provincial Lady in Wartime*, of making use of current events to create "the chronicles of that modest, fumbling, but curiously dry-witted heroine . . . the Diaries are a gentle joke on all her family, household, neighbours, and friends . . . and a clear laugh against herself . . . as more or less harmless and frequently ineffectual."[14] Here again is the characteristic Jane Austen *kindly but ironical* eye turned upon the author-as-writer herself.

Perhaps the most important autobiographical element of the Provincial Lady Diaries is E. M. Delafield's drawing on her husband, Paul Dashwood, and their circumstances for the portrait of Robert, the Provincial Lady's "consistently satirized" husband.[15] What is revealed is Everywoman's life with the husband who does not attend, transformed into wry humor.

A propos of the "Query: Does Robert, perhaps, take in what I say even when he makes no reply?" entry in the diary, critic Louis Kronenberger makes a remark which has also been leveled at the Jane Austen novels: that the male characters do not have a life of their own outside the prescribed comedy of manners interaction at various mealtimes and social occasions. Kronenberger asserts that "(The Diary) is extraordinarily feminine . . . it lacks the breadth and color of male participation in life."[16] It might be more accurate to say that the men in the Provincial Lady's life are not the kind who provide breadth and color; the Provincial Lady acknowledges that Robert's point of view is frequently different from her own, a gentle way of saying that his lack of animation lends new meaning to the word *dull*.

"(Query, mainly rhetorical: Why are non-professional women, if married and with children, so frequently referred to as 'leisured'? Answer comes there none.)" (DPL 244)

In a significant contemporary work that places Delafield in the *female aesthetic* tradition of Elaine Showalter's time line of women writers, Margaret Lawrence's *School of Femininity* (1936) describes *The Diary of a Provincial Lady* as one of those novels within the trend of "experimental portraiture of women." Lawrence characterizes heroines as one of three types: the "good pal," the "helpmeet woman," that is, one who "lives in honorable matrimony with a man, rearing his children, attending to his house," or a "sophisticated lady." She assigns the Provincial Lady to her rightful place, not as an apparent helpmeet woman, but as a sophisticated lady, because of the "sophisticated element" of thinking "her own thoughts as she goes through her days," and the fact that these are amusing thoughts. Lawrence's development of this premise is that the Provincial Lady has a husband who is "nice" about taking an interest in what goes on in his house and also "nice . . . about allowing his wife to write in her spare time, but he is only a man, and a woman has to have some outlet for her thoughts other than a man."[17] This leads to the revelation of the Provincial Lady's worth as an individual in her own right, coupled with the value of a woman's finding a means of self-expression:

> She is under no psychological strain about the unfair emotional relationship between men and women . . . but she wants to be . . . and must be entertaining . . . . The husband is varyingly attentive to the entertainment she provides . . . . He sticks and that is the main thing. He pays the bills . . . and she draws a picture of the life of an average couple together . . . after the long business of pulling together in harness has engrossed them to the exclusion of almost every other consideration.[18]

The *long business of pulling together in harness* has been alluded to by Mary Evans in *Jane Austen and the State*. The Diaries are continuing in the line of English literature in which both husband and wife, in terms of domesticity, had to contribute to the comfort of the home.[19] Evans also reminds us that such novels are set in the country, despite the cultural lure of London, because the small village was the center of English life in Jane Austen's time,[20] and it was still no less central and important over a century later when *The Diary of a Provincial Lady* was written and published. The Provincial Lady's purported feminist views give salt to the business of pulling together in harness:

> It rains, and presently Florence appears and says If I please, the water is coming in on the landing through the ceiling, and I say she had better go at once and find Robert—it occurs to me too late that this attitude is far from consistent with feminist views so often proclaimed by myself. (*PLA* 3)

Lawrence's analysis of the partnership in the first Diary is that "it is more important for a man to be able to pay the coal bills than to have power to drive a woman to distraction over the stray thoughts he may be thinking."[21] This catches the Provincial Lady's opinion of Love as the major consideration in a relationship—than which nothing matters more, according to her notorious friend, Pamela Pringle, but the Provincial Lady knows better: "Stifle strong inclination to reply that banking account, sound teeth and adequate servants matter a great deal more" (*PLL* 126). Earlier, when *helpmeet woman* Barbara Blenkinsop confesses to being engaged, saying that "she has always thought a true woman's highest vocation is home-making, and that the love of a Good Man is the crown of life," the Provincial Lady agrees, but comments to herself, "Discover that I do not" (*DPL* 129) and professes to be shocked by her own duplicity. Yes, the Provincial Lady is inherently realistic.

"He sticks, and that is the main thing" is surely a universal traditional consideration for the female partner. Lawrence's consideration is security, which is a traditional concern. She equates paying the bills, as the husband's responsibility in the unspoken bargain, with the sophisticated lady's own need to be entertaining, to "make it all seem extraordinarily interesting," but this division of labor fits only loosely the Provincial Lady's domestic arrangement. The responsibility for those coal bills or the rates seems to be hers, along with the overdraft at the bank. A comment by Vera Brittain about the Provincial Lady's creator bears this out: she quotes Lady Rhondda as saying that "all the Dashwood relatives keep telling Delafield she's not a good housekeeper & pity Paul (Paul Dashwood, EMD's husband) because *she* pays for everything."[22] A dichotomy exists here between the feminist expectations of Brittain, who claims that Delafield was "thoroughly immersed in the tradition of the submissive woman," giving way to her husband,[23] and the *sophisticated lady* attitude of Delafield's persona, according to Lawrence. The Provincial Lady's husband may "stick," but the inherent irony is that he provides precious little emotional support, while at the same time her wifely concern for inspiring fine feeling or her concern for its subsiding are playing a diminishing role in their relationship. Part of the answer may lie in the strictures of the topical writing of the Diaries, which fits the comedy of manners.

Delafield's conjectural use of her husband as the model for Robert bothered the Dashwood family to the extent that they would not authorize a biography of her until 1985, forty-two years after her death when, presumably, there would be few literary personages or others around who might remember her. Maurice McCullen, Delafield's biographer, suggests that this consideration might have been a reason the Diaries remained in comparative publishing and public, certainly critical, eclipse until they were reprinted in the early 1980s.[24]

"Life takes on entirely new aspect, owing to astonishing and unprecedented success of minute and unpretentious literary effort, published last December, and —incredibly —written by myself. Reactions of family and friends to this unforeseen state of affairs most interesting and varied." (PLL 1)

Contemporary reviews of the Diaries consistently augur a more lasting reputation for them. Literary critic Franklin P. Adams broke into rhyme in his panegyric to the Provincial Lady quoted on the cover of the second Diary, *The Provincial Lady in London*, original 1933 edition: "At home I yell and I also yell afield For this elegant book by E. M. Delafield." Louis Kronenberger was one of those who placed Delafield in the Jane Austen tradition. He describes her as a "skilful novelist of manners," observing that she has "an amused outlook on life, a feminine sharpness and a gift for not being taken in," a description that closely fits Priestley's lines on female humorists. His comment, "Mrs. Delafield observes her 'heroine' with the same keenness exercised by the heroine herself upon her neighbours,"[25] recalls Mr. Bennet's declaration to Elizabeth, "For what do we live, but to make sport for our neighbours, and laugh at them in our turn?" (*P&P* 315).

Kronenberger also finds in *The Diary of a Provincial Lady* a "shrewd satiric picture of English life" and concludes that "The world of this provincial lady is, in essence, the world that Jane Austen immortalized for all time, a world which has changed astonishingly little in a hundred years."[26] While this observation was made before World War II, a Labour government, and immigration of people with other mores changed the face of England, it still applies to both the rural structure of society and to the social traditions of the people who made up that society.

One of the most serious critical reviews of the Diaries, and one of the most helpful in linking E. M. Delafield with Jane Austen, was Henry Seidel Canby's 1933 review of *The Provincial Lady in London*. His analysis of Delafield allows her to be studied in the light of what J. B. Priestley had written just a few years before when using Jane Austen as his illustration of a female humorist:

> Why has she not had the resounding critical success which so many women writers less excellent than she have grown great upon? Because, I think, of her unpretentiousness, the unpretentiousness of one who, like Jane Austen, seems to write easily upon her lap, while others talk and clamor about her. She is some-what too ironic, too unsentimental, to get the reputation (which she deserves) of humorist, too delicate, too unpointed in her satire, to arouse fears or indignation, too much concerned with the humors of everyday manners as the best index of society, to interest the heavy-handed advocates of social change. She illustrates the difficulties of belonging to the Jane Austen school in the nineteen thirties.[27]

Canby is directly contrasting Delafield with those members of her literary circle who were "heavy-handed advocates of social change" in the Depression of the 1930s, and he acknowledges her ironic view of life admiringly. *The difficulties of belonging to the Jane Austen school in the nineteen thirties* not only reveals his disappointed expectations having to do with Delafield's lack of *critical* notoriety—she had a large and loyal *popular* following—but presages the declining appreciation of this subgenre of humor after Delafield's death in 1943, following the same pattern and the same fate as Benson's Lucia novels after his death in 1939. Nevertheless, Canby predicted perceptively that "her circle of readers will widen and that those she gets she will keep."[28] In late 1940, when *The Provincial Lady in Wartime* was published, a reviewer said that Delafield has a "claim to a high place in the delectable company of wits and originals using the English language as writers . . . like Chaucer, like Jane Austen,"[29] that is, nothing less than the most classic writers.

Although those predictions were not borne out in the short run, there continued to be fragments of solid criticism. In 1954, Delafield was recognized as having a lasting reputation on the English literary scene. Claiming that English fiction had been "in the doldrums" for the last twenty-five years, scholar Eric Gillett asked, "(during that time) how many characters have become or look like becoming part of our literary coinage?" And he placed "Elizabeth Delafield's 'Provincial Lady'" among those who achieved that status,[30] confirming that Delafield's renown, or at least Gillett's predilection for her memorable comic character, had survived into the 1950s. David Daiches, writing in 1958 about authors worthy of note at the time, comments about *The Diary of a Provincial Lady,* "(It) shows a lively yet cool observation at work. Her pose of studied objectivity yields its own kind of irony."[31] Daiches' succinct criticism defines Delafield in a way that re-confirms her place as a writer in the Jane Austen tradition.

After a gap of an entire generation, the Provincial Lady Diaries were reissued forty years later in paperback between 1980 and 1985, demonstrating both the prevailing interest in the work of women writers and the changed climate towards the acceptance of serious humor. Delafield's continuing vitality as part of English culture[32] is seen in her influence on at least one popular contemporary author, Miss Read (Dora Jessie Saint), whose more gentle humor has been recognized worldwide, and whose *Village School* (1955) has been required reading in secondary schools in England. In Miss Read's second Fairacre village novel, *Village Diary* (1957), three years after Eric Gillett's statement, Miss Read incorporates both an indirect quotation of Delafield's phraseology and recognizable analogies with the Provincial Lady's philosophy:

> Mrs. Pringle: "It's only True Love that matters!" Thus appealed to I found myself saying cautiously that I supposed it was important, but agreed privately with the Provincial Lady's secret feeling that a satisfactory bank account and good teeth matter a great deal more.[33]

In *No Holly for Miss Quinn* (1976), Miss Read also brings in the problem of the lack of time for the mother who would like not only to think out an idea, but to write it down, which is one of the Provincial Lady's motifs. Her character Miss Quinn, super secretary, gourmet cook, and now stand-in mother, is amused when her small nieces, nephew, and brother praise her lunch of bought, "instant" food: "And yet it had been relished. Perhaps there was a moral here, but there was certainly no time to pursue the thought, with the washing-up to be done, the girls to get ready, and Robin to put down for his afternoon nap."[34] That echoes the Provincial Lady's entry in her diary: "Brilliant, but nebulous outline of powerful Article for *Time and Tide* here suggests itself . . . . Failing article—for which time is lacking owing to departure of house-parlourmaid . . ." (*DPL* 105).

How did Delafield react to the immediate popularity of the Diaries? Upon the publication of the first one, *The Diary of a Provincial Lady*, she reports that she received many letters from readers who saw themselves in the people and circumstances of the Diary, bearing out the topical interest that the editor of *Time and Tide* originally had in mind, so that one friend "rather austerely" told her that "the only merit of the book lies in its universal appeal." One reader asked her in public, "How is Robert?" and another insisted that Delafield "wouldn't understand" how good the Diary was, leading her to this artistic apologia: "It was perhaps a little disconcerting to have so much praise showered upon a piece of work that I had done easily, quickly, and without much thought—whereas books at which I had worked a great deal harder remained comparatively unhonoured and unsung." Later that year her novel *Gay Life* appeared, "and was received with a chorus of moans that it was not another Diary."[35] Delafield, in short, believed that her other, more carefully crafted, social novels deserved more recognition; that the humorous Diaries were less worthy because they had been written "easily upon her lap," as Canby suggested, with the "unpretentiousness" of Jane Austen.

Unpretentiousness was not Jane Austen's private view of her own work. Her comments on *Pride and Prejudice* included, "I must confess that I think (Elizabeth Bennet) as delightful a creature as ever appeared in print, and how I shall be able to tolerate those who do not like *her* at least I do not know" (*L* 76 297); and, a satiric thrust, "the work is rather too light, and bright, and sparkling," showing that she professed to be aware of the advantage of some serious writing to offset the more brilliant, to "bring the reader with increased delight to the playfulness and epigrammatism of the general style" (*L* 77 299–300). Finally, perhaps the most endearing of her comments, showing how engaged she was with her characters, was made in a letter to her sister, Cassandra, during a visit to London in 1813 when *Pride and Prejudice* was published. She and her brother Henry went to the current art exhibitions.

> I was very well pleased . . . with a small portrait of Mrs. Bingley, excessively like her. I went in hopes of seeing one of her Sister, but there was no Mrs. Darcy . . . . Mrs. Bingley's (portrait) is exactly herself, size, shaped face, features & sweetness; there never was a greater likeness. She is dressed in a white gown, with green ornaments, which convinces me of what I had always supposed, that green was a favourite colour with her. I dare say Mrs. D. will be in Yellow . . . . *Monday even*[g].—We have been both to the Exhibition & Sir J. Reynolds',—and I am disappointed, for there was nothing like Mrs. D. at either. I can only imagine that Mr. D. prizes any Picture of her too much to like it should be exposed to the public eye.—I can imagine he w[d] have that sort of feeling—that mixture of Love, Pride & Delicacy. (*L* 80 309, 310)

Delafield's treatment of her own characters, so much of it drawn from life, is at once illuminated and caricatured in her introduction to Graham Laidler's *The British Character Studied and Revealed by Pont* (1938).

Although her comments are satirical, she seems to be describing, if not her characters, then the cross-section of her own audience. She begins, "Every Englishman is an average Englishman: it's a national characteristic . . . . To think is no part of their character. Instead of thoughts, the English have traditions. The tradition of the Home, for instance."[36] Illustrating this is the Provincial Lady's entry in her diary:

> (Robert) finds one can see the house from a hill near Plymouth and he would like me to have a look at it. Shall never wholly understand advantages to be derived from seeing any place from immense distance instead of close at hand, as could easily be done from the tennis lawn without any exertion at all—but quite realise that masculine point of view on this question, as on so many others, differs from my own . . . . (*PLL* 160–1)

As to the average Englishman, Delafield continues, "The English neither possess, nor wish to possess, any imagination at all. They only possess, to a very high degree, the quality of faith as defined by the school boy: Believing what you know to be untrue."[37] Delafield includes on this list of beliefs that "listening to the wireless is meritorious but reading a novel is waste of time."[38] At a frivolous estimate one might say that the nine o'clock news appears without fail in every modern novel with any pretension to being part of the domestic comedy of manners:

> I listen for some time to unsympathetic female voice from the wireless . . . switch off wireless just as unsympathetic female branches off into something about wild violets . . . and presently discover that I have missed the nine o'clock news altogether. Robert also discovers this, and is again not pleased. (*PLA* 7)

Although the Provincial Lady's new women acquaintances in London discuss books that cannot have been "out for more than five minutes" ("How on earth do Pamela and her friends achieve conversation about books which I am perfectly certain they have none of them read?" (*PLL* 154)), the average Englishman is different. Old Mrs. Blenkinsop has been apt to refer ostentatiously to a *Life of Lord Beaconsfield* and Shakespeare, but an apparent Philistine now lives with her. "We touch on literature in general—Cousin Maude says that books collect dust, anyway, and whisks away inoffensive copy of *Time and Tide* with which old Mrs. B. is evidently solacing herself . . ." (*DPL* 208), and, before the trip to a literary conference, "July 14th.—Question of books to be taken abroad undecided till late hour last night. Robert says, Why take any?" (*DPL* 213). And in wartime, the crowning indignity:

> Literary Agent says: Still, no doubt I realise that now—if ever—is the time when books are going to be read, and of course, whilst there are so few places of entertainment open, and people go out so little in the evenings, they will really be almost *forced* to take to books. (*PLW* 300)

Perhaps the most important of these unquestioning beliefs is, "Most Englishmen if forced into analysing their own creed—which Heaven forbid—are convinced that God is an Englishman—probably educated at Eton"[39]; therefore, it follows, in the comedy of manners, that His representatives will be the same. Jane Austen's Edmund Bertram has been to Eton and Oxford; Mr. Collins only "kept the necessary terms" without realizing any benefit from them, and most of the other clergymen in the Benson, Delafield, and Thirkell novels are as Delafield's average Englishman would have them.

"Feel that if this is to be Our Vicar's only contribution towards the solution of the problem, he might just as well have stayed at home—but naturally do not impart this opinion to his wife" (*DPL* 142).

Whether educated at Eton or not, clergymen have proven to be a major ingredient of the domestic comedy of manners and deserve their own defense. Jane Austen's clergymen are not necessarily seen as dealing with everyday concerns, except for Mr. Elton, who is good to the poor—Emma and Harriet Smith meet him on a charitable errand—and he discusses parish business with Mr. Knightley, Mr. Weston, and Mr. Cole. When Delafield's Our Vicar is summoned to "give impartial advice to all parties," his words, reported by Our Vicar's Wife, are regarded by the Provincial Lady as so ambivalent as to be ludicrous:

> Yes, Yes—he is all in favor of young folk living their own lives, whilst at the same time he feels that a mother's claims are sacred, and although he realises the full beauty of self-sacrifice, yet on the other hand no one knows better than he does that the devotion of a Good Man is not to be lightly relinquished. (*DPL* 142)

This is followed by the Provincial Lady's own comment, which always constitutes the true, wry humor of the Diaries: "Feel that if this is to be Our Vicar's only contribution towards the solution of the problem, he might just as well have stayed at home—but naturally do not impart this opinion to his wife" (*DPL* 142). This swift sketch portrays the Vicar's counsel as of little earthly use to his parishioners. Nonetheless, Our Vicar has a role: if Delafield is to be considered a traditionalist in her view of women, as Margaret McDowell suggests, he, not Robert, is the true touchstone of tradition—of propriety—for the Provincial Lady's actions. These include her not showing a new décolleté evening dress to his wife, immediately putting down on her book club list the book he has "declared very painful and unnecessary" (*DPL* 160), and acknowledging that the discussion about how to raise funds during Lent becomes "much less elastic" upon the arrival of Our Vicar's wife (*DPL* 74).

Kronenberger's critical comment that Delafield's characters are "types too true to form" is helpful because it is made in the context of her writing and redefines this writing within the Jane Austen tradition:

> Fortunately, she has her justification: the novelist of manners, the satirist, may fairly claim the right to cling to the recognizable, for his chief aim is to portray not individual character but social life; and social life, which cannot abide anomaly, is a record of what is most generally true. [40]

Delafield's words for Pont confirm Kronenberger's statement, illustrating how, even why, she creates her characters for the Provincial Lady Diaries: they are less local or stock characters than universals. That her "average

Englishman" is a universal is attested to by her assertion that "Robert was intended to represent the average English husband, and judging from every comment ever made about him he did so."[44] Delafield illustrates her earlier description of her audience as readers who saw themselves in the people and circumstances of *The Diary of a Provincial Lady* with, "It is a startling and salutary thought that most of us are so very much alike that we all recognize one another at sight, and that some even go so far as to recognize ourselves."[42]

"(Query: Are Competition Editors always sound on questions of literary merit? Judgement possibly becomes warped through overwork.)" (DPL 49)

The lapse in both popular and critical interest in the comedy of manners novels of the early twentieth century from the end of World War II until the 1980s has been attributed to the more serious social climate. Another reason may be the lack of regard for *words* themselves as a source of humor. In an increasingly proletarian society, other, more seemingly practical things are valued more; in general, language—irony, metonymy, synecdoche—has not been one of them. Some of Delafield's use of language is similar to that of Jane Austen, particularly the unexpected sequence that brings humor. One example of this is found first in *Pride and Prejudice*:

> (Elizabeth) felt, that years of happiness could not make Jane or herself amends, for moments of such painful confusion . . . . Yet the misery, for which years of happiness were to offer no compensation, received soon afterwards material relief, from observing how much the beauty of her sister re-kindled the admiration of her former lover. (337)

and, a second instance, in the more serious *Mansfield Park*:

> Long, long would it be ere Miss Crawford's name passed his lips again, or she could hope for a renewal of such confidential intercourse as had been. It *was* long. They reached Mansfield on Thursday, and it was not till Sunday evening that Edmund began to talk to her on the subject. (453)

Delafield carries on this technique with the denouement of a broken engagement. "They have, says Barbara in tears, parted For Ever, and Life is Over, and will I take the Guides' Meeting for her tonight" (*DPL* 135).

She also employs metonymy in the way some writers use identifying names. In describing a morning wasted at the registry office hoping to interview a cook, the Provincial Lady lists the *dramatis personae* as "offensive-looking woman in orange *beret*, who sits at desk," hereafter referred to as "orange *beret*," and "harassed-looking lady in transparent pink mackintosh (who) trails in . . . . The pink mackintosh, like Queen Victoria, is not amused" (*PLL* 56,7). Doubtless this one-dimensional identification flattens a character, but it also provides recognition, usually humorous, because the succinct descriptions are frequently incongruous with the role, dignity, or even occupation of the person so described.

Much of the humor of the Diaries depends upon Delafield's ironic view, the *kindly but ironic* eye with which the Provincial Lady sees herself. Not surprisingly, the greater part of this situation relates, as it would today, to the tension caused by conflicting calls on the time and interests of the writer who is also wife and mother. Her subject soon appears in the first and most domestic Diary, which Delafield described as illustrating "the circumstances of almost all of us who live in the country on small means, and struggle with children." There the Provincial Lady, as Delafield's persona, notes, "Mentally reserve the question for bringing forward on next occasion of finding myself in intellectual society. This, however, seems at the moment remote in the extreme" (*DPL* 49); and "Query, mainly rhetorical: Why are non-professional women, if married and with children, so frequently referred to as 'leisured'? Answer comes there none" (*DPL* 244). In *The Provincial Lady in London*, the Provincial Lady, who has achieved notoriety for her first novel and received a small inheritance, acquires a tiny flat in London, a "room of her own" to write in. The motif continues, even when the Provincial Lady can afford to take the family to Southern France for a holiday:

I make mental note to the effect that the young are definitely dependent on routine and have dim idea of evolving interesting little article on the question, to be handsomely paid by daily Press—but nothing comes of it. (*PLL* 91).

A further illustration from this period also demonstrates the humor of the unexpected sequence, exaggeration, and dry incongruity of subject:

(Mem.: Wifely intuition very peculiar and interesting, and apparently subject to laws at present quite unapprehended by finite mind. Material here for very deep, possibly scientific, article. Should like to make preliminary notes, but laundry calls, and concentrate instead on total omission of everything except thirty-four handkerchiefs and one face-towel from clothes-basket. Decide to postpone article until after the holidays.) (*PLL* 174)

After the holidays everywhere means that the children will have gone back to school— here, to boarding school. In the third Diary, when organizing the children for school and herself for her lecture tour in America, the Provincial Lady once more descends abruptly from fantasy to practicality:

Decide that the Modern Girl has been maligned. Possible material here for interesting little article on Preconceived Opinions in regard to Unfamiliar Types? Have vague idea of making a few notes on these lines, but this finally resolves itself into a list of minor articles required by Robin and Vicky, headed, as usual, by Tooth Paste. (*PLA* 30).

This entry achieves a neat play on words with *article*. The dry, practical tone of her diary entries amused her readers, and her refrain of "Answer comes there none" to some of her own more imponderable queries immediately caught on, to become *in* language.[43]

The examples illustrate the underlying tension between her role as a professional writer and her role as a wife and mother, but they do not give a sufficient picture of the Provincial Lady or Delafield as part of a literary circle in London. There is yet another side to the tug-of-war between the Provincial Lady's two worlds. In 1926, Winifred Holtby, the novelist best known for *South Riding*, met Delafield at a lunch for new contributors to *Time and Tide*. She reported to a correspondent that "EMD is very thin, thirtyish, smart, dark and married, with small children who occupy her a good deal,"[44] from which it may be inferred that Delafield was known to them both through her work. Others in the *Time and Tide* circle also were married, and Vera Brittain, at least, had two children. At the same time, most were feminists, and Holtby's comment *with small children who occupy her a good deal* should not be read as a sympathetic one. Disapproval of the Provincial Lady's ambivalence towards living in London is brought out in the Diaries in conversations with her feminist friend Emma: "Dear old friend . . . and author of many successful plays says, Fancy seeing me here! and have I broken away at last? I say, No, certainly not, and suggest dinner" (*PLL* 30). Later, Emma invites the Provincial Lady to join her on a camping trip to Wales, saying that she "lives on" bananas and milk chocolate:

> Associations with the last words lead me to reply absently that the children would like it, at which Emma seems hurt and enquires whether I intend to spend my life between the nursery and the kitchen? The only possible answer to this is that I *like* it, and discussion becomes animated and rather painful. (*PLL* 38, 9).

Even after gratifying success in London and the companionship of intellectual equals unobtainable in Devonshire, the Provincial Lady notes,

> I . . . explain that I am returning to the country in a few hours' time. What, shrieks Emma, leaving London? Am I mad? Do I intend to spend the whole of the rest of my life pottering about the kitchen, and seeing that Robert gets his meals punctually, and that the children don't bring muddy boots into the house? Reply quite curtly and sharply: Yes, I do . . . . (*PLL* 280).

The question of happiness in marriage is different in degree from that of domestic thraldom, and that is the third theme in the fabric of these extracts from the Diaries. Vera Brittain describes Delafield as "depressed because she uses her Bloomsbury flat so little that she'll have to give it up," that it "'didn't make for happy married life' if she went up to town very much," and concludes, ". . . it makes one feel that writing women oughtn't to marry . . . ." [45] Delafield has the Provincial Lady make a typical remark on this basic incompatibility:

> Very, very distinguished Novelist approaches me . . . . She says that she can only write between twelve at night and four in the morning, and not always then. When she cannot work, she plays the organ. Should much like to ask if she is married. (*PLL* 62)

This situation certainly is not new to the contemporary woman, but Delafield allows the Provincial Lady, who also has had a literary success and is able to spend part of her time in London, to cast that *kindly but ironical* eye upon herself and to record in her current Diary an additional fictional comment that seems close to the bone for Delafield's own marriage:

> Pay a call on Robert's Aunt Mary . . . (she) hopes that my writing does not interfere with home life and its many duties, and I hope so too, but in spite of this joint aspiration, impression prevails that we are mutually dissatisfied with one another. We part, and I go away thinking that I have been a failure. (*PLL* 229).

Along the way the Provincial Lady makes what is without a doubt one of the most humorous and, under the circumstances, most revealing gaffes in the Diaries, with an addendum that equals it:

> I am moved to explain—perhaps rather thoughtlessly—that the most wonderful thing in the world must be to be a childless widow—but this is met by unsympathetic silence by Robert, which recalls me to myself, and impels me to say that that isn't in the *least* what I meant. (*DPL* 198, 9)

Delafield's irony is what sets her work apart from that of the other, more earnest feminist writers of those two decades, and partially explains Kronenberger's comment that there were difficulties to writing in the Jane Austen tradition in the 1930s. Some of the work of her circle has been rediscovered at the end of the twentieth century: Vera Brittain's *Testimony Of Youth* (1932) was made into a BBC television series, and Rose Macaulay, Sylvia Townsend Warner, and Rebecca West continue to have a following.

The question of Delafield as a feminist and her expressions of this philosophy becomes complex if she is judged by the active socialist bent of some members of her literary circle. Critic Carolyn Heilbrun describes this group as "vital proponents of feminism, active in many causes, (and) professionally committed."[46] Delafield lives the philosophy by having an independent life. In addition, in the guise of author-as-writer she gives further indication of the nature of her convictions through the words and actions of the Provincial Lady. She is successfully prevailed upon by her young daughter, Vicki, to be allowed to go away to school, instead of being automatically kept at home to be taught by Mademoiselle. At other times the Provincial Lady is furious with Lady Boxe, the inhabitant of the Big House of the neighborhood, finding her condescending, very much in the way Jane Austen's *Emma* finds Mrs. Elton insufferable, except there the roles are reversed, as Mrs. Elton is the social inferior. The Provincial Lady's political views, which are not those of Lady Boxe, are shown through an exchange with "Lady B.," in which the latter asks the Provincial Lady if she will help at a bazaar "in aid of the Party Funds." The Provincial Lady denies sympathy for the (Tory) Party, Lady B. professes to be surprised and brings forward the Russians for consideration, to which the Provincial Lady retorts, "Look at Unemployment," and "relieves (her) feelings by waving small red flag belonging to Vicky . . . and saying *A la lanterne!* as chauffeur drives off" with Lady B. (*DPL* 82, 3). Delafield's readers of this topical material must have recognized the provoking elements of the class system that remained a fact of life at the beginning of the 1930s and that was protested by her literary circle.

"September 1st, 1939.—Enquire of Robert whether he does not think that, in view of times in which we live, diary of daily events might not be of ultimate historical value to posterity. He replies that It Depends." (PLW 1)

In *The Provincial Lady in Wartime*, Delafield's last Diary, the class system is still intact in the early days of the war and Lady Boxe is still overbearing. Delafield's views are reflected by the Provincial Lady, who after one of Lady B.'s calls records that she has confided to Aunt Blanche, the elderly relative running the house in Devonshire while the Provincial Lady looks for war work in London, that

> much as I dislike everything I have ever heard or read about Stalin and his regime, there are times when I should feel quite prepared to join (the) Communist party. Aunt Blanche only answers, with great common sense, that she does not think I had better say anything of that kind in front of Robert . . . . (221,2).

That, of course, is the classic domestic comedy of manners! Despite an overwhelming world crisis, away from the bureaucratic atmosphere of London, where the Provincial Lady is ineffectual in having her offer to serve in the war effort accepted, Aunt Blanche still has both butter and honey in abundance on the tea table and is apt to defer to Lady Boxe, who is still patronizing. The Provincial Lady resorts to threats of Communism, a classless society, to deal with Aunt Blanche—only to be put in her place by a traditionally minded woman who believes that husbands' opinions count.

The Provincial Lady in Wartime is probably the most topical of the Diaries. In discussing Delafield after her death, Lady Rhondda, the editor of *Time and Tide*, uses an excerpt from the first three pages of that last Diary as her main example in calling Delafield's writing evocative of a particular time, capturing a mood. First of all the Provincial Lady defines her intentions:

> September 1st, 1939—Enquire of Robert whether he does not think that, in view of the times in which we live, diary of daily events might not be of ultimate value to posterity. He replies that It Depends. Explain that I do not mean events of national importance, which may safely be left to the Press, but only chronicle of ordinary English citizen's reactions to war which now appears inevitable. Robert's only reply—if reply it can be called—is to enquire whether I am really certain that Cook takes a medium size in gas-masks. Personally, he should have thought that a large, if not out-size, was indicated. Am forced to realize that Cook's gas-mask is intrinsically of greater importance than problematical contribution to literature by myself . . . . (1)

The whole passage about Cook's somewhat skittishly humoring Robert, trying on gas masks and wanting to get back to her fish cakes, ends with Robert's comment, incomprehensible to the Provincial Lady, "That's a good job done." In 1947 Lady Rhondda writes, "How that takes one back to an almost forgotten mood. One thought that one had mislaid the feelings of those weeks but as one reads, the very flavour of them comes back. We were not all ARP wardens or cooks but we all have our memories."[47] Lady Rhondda's words demonstrate that Delafield's writing, because it was topical, has become a part of social history for members of that vanished world.

The Provincial Lady in Wartime, a *chronicle of (an) ordinary English citizen's reactions to war*, was written in the early months of World War II, the period called "the People's War" or "the Phoney War," and published in 1940. In portraying the comedy of manners, both domestic and beyond, under serious circumstances, the novel is neither anticlimactic nor repetitious of the earlier Diaries. The wartime Diary is careful to have the Provincial Lady keep the same somewhat ineffectual persona and the locals, such as Lady B., show their true colors, whether liberal or selfish, in the crisis. What is fresh is the addition of the support group of like-minded people in London, not all of them women and some not old enough to be considered "feminists" in the political sense of the earlier Diaries. Another difference is Delafield's more satirical tone in describing the Provincial Lady's frustrating encounters with the Ministry of Information. That body has created an impenetrable bureaucratic maze of ever-shifting offices, and one person whom she successfully tracks down calls her "All You People" and tells her to go on writing novels, just as though the war didn't exist, for in all likelihood "people will take to reading when they find there's absolutely nothing else to do" (*PLW* 266).

This portrayal is at once the best representation of high morale on the home front and the best boost to that morale. The domestic comedy of manners has become social history. Upper-middle-class England, liberal, informed, thoughtful, is portrayed at the time by *The Provincial Lady in Wartime*, Angela Thirkell's novels *Northbridge Rectory* and *Cheerfulness Breaks In*, Jan Struther's novel *Mrs. Miniver*, and the letters and journals of novelists Margaret Kennedy and Barbara Pym. *The Provincial Lady in Wartime* completes this group with its similarity of situation and outlook to what those popular authors, all women, were writing about. They are revealed as more idealistic and at the same time more pessimistic about the future of England, and of their class. Their works of both fiction and non-fiction have given us local pictures of evacuating children from the danger zones of London and the Channel coast to Devonshire, providing and illustrating the accounts and statistics in such later sourcebooks as *The Phoney War* and *The People's War*. For example, almost everyone in the country must cope with evacuées. The Provincial Lady and family make room for children who do not appear and then receive children who do, but whose mothers do not like the country. The billeting officer's hands are full, with "evacuées from all parts of the country . . . hastening back to danger zones as rapidly as possible, as being infinitely preferable to rural hospitality (or) the country hostesses proving inadequate and clamouring for the removal of their guests" (24).

This Diary reflects the reactions not only of the Provincial Lady's family circle in wartime but also of her wider circle in wartime London. She takes satiric aim at overstatement, misinformation, generalization, and exaggeration. Her targets are self-important people at the Ministry of Information and outside: one vaunted luncheon guest, with supposed inside information, is captured forever in "Monsieur Gitnik resembles fourteenth-rate crystal-gazer, probably with business premises in mews off Tottenham Court Road" (135).

When the reissue of *The Provincial Lady in Wartime* in 1985 brought the book to the critics' attention, we note that Margaret McDowell considers the Diary as lacking in humor. She sees Delafield as satirizing "the sentimental patriotism of volunteers, their bureaucratic inefficiency, and their self-importance."[48]   Satirizing the self-importance of the young woman Commandant who has No Time to eat, yes; but that *sentimental patriotism*, in reality far more often practical than sentimental, shows a whole spectrum of English men and women responding to, often anticipating, the trumpet call to duty. Those whom satirizes are entrenched in the civil service and glory in their chains. Epitomizing this group is her character Mr. Weatherby, whom the Provincial Lady characteristically refers to as "Agrippa" after she notes a resemblance between him and that august, historical personage. When the Provincial Lady invites the Weatherbys to a little sherry party, Mrs. Weatherby declines for them:

> (because) anything may happen, at any moment anywhere—and if it does, I shall of course understand that he will be Tied. Absolutely tied. Reply that I do, and refuse to dwell on foolish and flippant fancy of Agrippa fastened up by stout cords, dealing with national emergency from his office desk. (297)

Time and Tide was delighted to have Delafield—"EMD"—back in its pages with the weekly series of *The Provincial Lady in Wartime*. In *Punch*, December 1939, she mocks the Ministry of Information's adjuration to All You People to "go on writing as though (the war) didn't exist" (*PLW* 237) by telling her readers not to read newspapers or listen to the radio but to return to good books, because "A war spent in reading, is a well-spent war."[49]   It is clear that the Provincial Lady has long since become a sought-after member of the disparaged group of All You People, and the Diary ends on a gratified note:

> November 21st (1939)—Am startled as never before on receiving notification that my services as a writer are required, and may even take me abroad. Am unable to judge whether activities will permit of my continuing a diary but prefer to suppose that they will be of too important a nature. (*PLW* 312)

Those concluding remarks ring with a forgivable note of innocent self-importance and an equal amount of self-mockery, the result of the *kindly but ironical* eye with which these comedy of manners writers view their favorite characters.

"(Query: Does this denote irrational hope of sudden and complete transformation in personal appearance? If so, can only wonder that so much faith should meet with so little reward." (PLL 193)

Personal appearance—her wardrobe; her hairstyle—is one of her concerns, and there is far more about dress, and the consequent ironies of attire inappropriate for the occasion, than is shown by any of the Jane Austen heroines. The close connection between reality and artistry, or semiautobiography, as Lady Rhondda termed the Diaries, is seen in and around the Provincial Lady's entry for June 9 (1932), about serving on the committee for a party to be given by *Time and Tide*: "I get myself a new frock for the occasion," and on June 16th, ". . . frock very successful" (*PLL* 230). Vera Brittain, part of Delafield's literary circle, also writing about the *Time and Tide* reception on June 16, completes the picture: "Delafield most cleverly & effectively dressed in a saffron-coloured 'smock' frock—very *chic* and yet '*Provincial Lady*-ish.'"[50] Before her emergence on the London literary scene, the Provincial Lady establishes the tone about appearance. After she has been talked into having her hair "touched up," she mocks herself with "Think seriously of keeping a hat on all through lunch" (*DPL* 69).

"(Mem.: A meal the most satisfactory way of entertaining any guest. Should much like to abridge the interval between tea and dinner—or else to introduce supplementary collation in between.)" (DPL 45)

In recent years food has been the newly popular subject for critical discussion, and it makes a beguiling topic for demonstrating humor in the comedy of manners. Food can hardly be left out when invoking the Jane Austen tradition, especially now that Margaret Drabble, in the name of feminist sensibility, has plumped for "supper at Longbourn with Mrs. Bennet any day (rather) than a soft-boiled egg with Mr. Woodhouse."[51] Food is an inseparable part of the routine—four times a day at least for the lady of the house—and is tied to both propriety, appropriateness, and hospitality. For example, Robert's slightly burnt breakfast porridge will be redeemed by the ham ordered against the Christmas visit of his brother, William, and William's wife, Angela. Commenting on the ritual and reason for tea—making the best of people she does not care for all that much—the Provincial Lady notes: "(Mem.: A meal the most satisfactory way of entertaining any guest. Should much like to abridge the interval between tea and dinner—or else to introduce supplementary collation in between)" (*DPL* 45).

Food illustrates the Provincial Lady's admitted lack of housekeeping expertise. When the Provincial Lady would like to impress Lady Boxe, the Diary reads, "Tea is brought in—and Cook has, as usual, carried out favourite labour-saving device of three sponge cakes and one bun jostling each other on the same plate" (*DPL* 159). More important, her remarks about the traditional English Sunday Lunch, a constant in the Diaries, show her restlessness with conventions: "Receive telephone invitation to lunch with the Frobishers on Sunday. I accept, less because I want to see them than because a change from domestic roast beef and gooseberry-tart always pleasant; moreover, absence makes work lighter for the servants," which is followed by the typical "(Mem.: Candid and intelligent self-examination as to motive, etc., often leads to very distressing revelations)" (*DPL* 171).

Once the Provincial Lady has left Devonshire and achieved London, away from the domestic routine, she asserts herself, and records what to Robert has the dimensions of a revolution: "Return to roast beef—underdone—and plates not very hot. I say boldly that I think roast beef every Sunday is a mistake—why not chicken, or even mutton? but at this everyone looks aghast, and Robert asks What next, in Heaven's name?"

(*PLL* 111). Perhaps best of all, at one point she is able to override her arch-enemy, Cook, about sandwiches for a picnic: "I perceive that the moment has come for taking up absolutely firm stand with Cook, and surprise us both by suddenly saying Nonsense, she must order chicken . . . I pursue advantage . . . Cook utterly vanquished, and I leave the kitchen triumphant" (*DPL* 254). This does not last, however ("never thought it would"), and on her trip to America later she refers to the high standard of American cooking, especially the "excellent coffee," and notes the necessity for telling Cook this.

The crowning remark, recapturing the Provincial Lady's lifetime dilemmas, is her culinary, philosophical, and pragmatic Diary entry: "I decide that almost every sorrow can probably be assuaged by a respectable meal. (Mem.: Try to remember this and act upon it next time life appears to be wholly intolerable.)" (*PLA* 120)

3

Angela Thirkell

"Mrs. Morland . . . was stopped by seven or eight (convalescent soldiers) with sixpenny copies of her books which they wanted her to sign, offering fountain-pens and pencils . . . from silver-cased to indelible." (GU 278)

The writer whose novels are closest to those of Jane Austen in terms of young heroines and heroes is Angela Thirkell. She is regarded as in the direct line from Jane Austen through the gentle humor of *Cranford*. Born into an artistic tradition, she was a granddaughter of Burne-Jones, daughter of Professor George Mackail, sister of *Greenery Street* novelist Denis Mackail, and cousin of Kipling. Her second marriage took her to Australia, where she found an opportunity to exercise her literary ambitions writing a number of short pieces. She returned to England and immediately found her artistic voice with *Wild Strawberries* (1934), the first of her popular novels about three or four families in a country village. Unlike E. F. Benson and E. M. Delafield, Thirkell had no illusions about a talent for more "serious" writing. Her persona, author Laura Morland, mocks herself for writing "good bad novels," all of which, she claims, are alike.

"Laura herself had no illusions as to her books being, in any high sense of the word, literature, but she knew they had an appeal . . . ." (HR 17)

Critical reviews of 60 years ago place Thirkell's novels in the Jane Austen tradition: *Pomfret Towers* (1938) "has in a lesser degree the keen quiet humor . . . the light satirical touch and the enjoyment of human

absurdities we always associate with (Jane Austen)."[1] The same criticism
applies to *The Brandons* (1939), where Louise Field, reviewer for the *New
York Times*, redefines the comedy of manners as understood in the 1930s
and explains Thirkell's identification with the Jane Austen tradition:

> Social satire unblemished by spite is one of the rarest types of fiction . . . a
> genuine delight in the twists and inconsistencies of the human comedy . . . . To
> laugh at 'follies and nonsense, whims and inconsistencies' as pleasantly and
> gayly as Elizabeth Bennet did requires an unusual mixture of humor, quick
> perception and mental maturity. While Angela Thirkell does not rank with
> Elizabeth Bennet, or rather with Elizabeth's creator and prototype, Jane Austen,
> she belongs in that enchanting company.[2]

Thirkell wrote *Before Lunch* (1939) without regard to the threat of war,
and Field cites the reality of the times to make clear what has periodically
happened to the popularity, even the credibility, of the comedy of manners:

> No literary tradition is more difficult to carry on in these harassed days than the
> Jane Austen . . . . To take a group of altogether ordinary people, yet make
> them at once sympathetic, interesting, and highly amusing, is asking a great deal
> of any modern writer . . . with what apparent ease (Thirkell) accomplishes all
> this, aided always by her own witty or ironic comments.[3]

Thirkell's next works, her five wartime novels—*Cheerfulness Breaks In*
(1941), *Marling Hall* and *Northbridge Rectory* (1942), *Growing Up* (1944),
and *The Headmistress* (1945)—plunge the reader into war on the home front.
Reviewing *Northbridge Rectory*, Field reflects the American public's
predominantly Anglophile leanings at the time in her comment, "Through
all the book there glows a steady light; that beacon light of courage Great
Britain holds on high." [4] In *Growing Up*, soldiers at a convalescent home
bombard author Mrs. Morland with admiring questions and requests for her
autograph on the books they produce. This high point parallels Thirkell's
own gratifying letters from British soldiers of all levels, including prisoners
of war, saying that her novels depicted the England they were defending.
In 1945 critic Orville Prescott agrees, terming Thirkell "a novelist who
occupies a niche in my private pantheon just a little below that of Mr.

Winston Churchill as a symbol of enduring British virtues."[5] We may not be aware that during World War I, Jane Austen's novels also enjoyed an enormous popularity with English officers and enlisted men alike, a popularity celebrated in Rudyard Kipling's short story "The Janeites."

A later portrayal of Thirkell as "snobbish," in a memoir (1985) by her son Graham McInnes,[6] has surprised long-time Thirkell readers. In Robertson Davies' Introduction to that memoir, he particularizes the allegation of *snobbish*, describing Thirkell as having "a very English sense of class and snobbery" in Australia.[7] The comedy of manners is characteristically played out by a social spectrum that includes, as Jane Austen's heroine Elizabeth Bennet is justified in saying to Lady Catherine de Bourgh, both her father and Mr. Darcy as *gentlemen* (*P&P* 356), and as Thirkell's Jane Gresham knows, "the Duke of Omnium at one end and Robin Dale, the crippled schoolmaster, at the other, (who) were in essentials equal" (*MB* 175). In her novels written before World War II, Thirkell colors the domestic life of that class in a hazy, sunny, cricket-game afternoon glow: the male characters are glorified as young, strong, and handsome, and the women are eccentrically charming and extremely well dressed, but only marginally sensible.

McInnes's personal view diverges from the critical view of Thirkell that was established in the 1930s and 1940s, as being in the comedy of manners tradition of "laugh(ing) at the faults and failings, vanities and absurdities of her characters, but her laughter is never harsh. For with very few exceptions these people have one trait in common: they are fundamentally kind."[8] Field offers two illustrations: in *High Rising* (1934), "George Knox was, like most of the other people in Angela Thirkell's delightful world, a very kindly person,"[9] and in *Before Lunch*, "the autocratic Lady Bond sacrificed her nerves and convenience year after year to give a holiday to an exasperating friend who was bearing genteel poverty very courageously in London."[10] In the latter novel Lord Bond has "an extremely kind heart and looked after his tenants with an amount of real kindness" (88).

"Each (young woman) made it a point of honour to pretend she could not touch anything that the other liked, so that neither got more than half of David's delightful meal." (WS 106)

Food plays a significant role in the comedy of manners. In 1945 Orville Prescott reported that some critics judged Thirkell's novels as "mild as milk and as exciting as rice pudding."[11] It was meant to be an unflattering comment, but in the metaphor of today, the novels may be considered "comfort food," because of those reassuring associations with rice pudding. In the Austen novels, for example, Emma encounters "Mr. John Knightley returning from the daily visit to Donwell, with his two eldest boys, whose healthy, glowing faces shewed all the benefit of a country run, and seemed to ensure a quick dispatch of the roast mutton and rice pudding they were hastening home for" (*E* 109). The importance of food is unavoidable: the lady of the house has been responsible for the provision of the food for four meals a day, as well as for the enjoyment of those eating it.

In Benson's Tilling, food to precede or follow bridge games is usually a matter of competition among the hostesses, not least in the *appearance* of plenty; similarly, Delafield has the Provincial Lady comment on the powers of a good meal. Thirkell's chatelaines also hold themselves responsible for a good meal, whether in peace or war, for that is when the families and their guests come together: the dinner parties and the opportunity for socializing, breakfast and, of course, tea, so much so that Isabelle Mallet, reviewing *Growing Up* late in the war, says that Thirkell's novels, because of being regarded as typically British, have "a general aroma of buttered crumpets."[12]

In some sense, food in the Austen novels has a role separate from that of mealtime. In *Mansfield Park* Mrs. Grant's turkeys, legs of mutton, and apricot tarts are prepared for the gratification of her husband's epicurean appetite, offending Mrs. Norris's native parsimony. In the familiar and humorous example of the attentive hostess, Emma Woodhouse "allowed her father to talk—but supplied her visitors in a much more satisfactory style," with all the good things that have been chosen with an eye to the tastes of the older ladies, in response to Mr. Woodhouse's celebrated recommendations around the table: "Mrs. Bates . . . an egg boiled very soft is not unwholesome . . . . Miss Bates, let Emma help you to a *little* bit of tart . . . . I do not advise the custard. Mrs. Goddard, what say you to *half* a glass of wine?" (*E* 24, 25).

Novelist and editor Margaret Drabble wrote for the Jane Austen Society that the reason for her choice of "supper at Longbourn with Mrs. Bennet (rather) than a soft-boiled egg with Mr. Woodhouse"[13] was that Mrs. Bennet wanted to provide an appropriate background for her daughters—a lavish display of soup, venison "roasted to a turn," and "remarkably well done partridges," a supper that would be "good enough for a man, on whom she had such anxious designs" (*P&P* 338). When Elizabeth Bennet makes a morning call at Pemberley, Mr. Darcy has provided a more delicate collation of "beautiful pyramids of grapes, nectarines, and peaches" (*P&P* 268). Critic Maggie Lane's recent interpretation of the symbolism of food in the Jane Austen novels suggests a special significance for this fruit: "Just as (Elizabeth) is beginning to acknowledge Darcy's real humanity, she is given this sign of the ripeness of his affection, which is no longer the arid and emotionally immature infatuation against his better judgement which had got the better of him at Rosings."[14] Further, this is the only time in her novels that a Jane Austen heroine even takes note of what is being offered to eat.

Food has various roles in the Austen novels, but the establishment of mealtime as central meeting place for the family, as well as the time to welcome a guest, is stronger for Thirkell. In a convivial moment at the Bonds' post-Agricultural Show dinner when discussing cousins and connections by marriage, Lady Bond's guest Miss Starter "quite forgot her diet and took melted butter and a piece of ordinary toast, both of which were wellknown to be death to her" (*BL* 272). Also, when discussing "Honorables" with Mr. Palmer at that dinner, she "ate some ice pudding, a delicacy absolutely forbidden by her physician" (274), affirming the hospitality and solicitude of the hostess. Afternoon tea frequently is an oasis after a parched day. The tea is always hot and fresh, with the hostesses making sure that it is replenished.

Thirkell's hostesses are hospitable by definition, and Thirkell does not mock the housewifery of her chatelaines; she applauds and honors them, with the exception of Mrs. Tebben (*AF*), who stands out as a homemaking failure: her favorite economy is stewed, black, tepid tea. Mrs. Tebben does have catering concerns, but she does not know how to make tea, and she should be back at the university, where her real interests lie. In *The Brandons*, Cook and Hattie are able to get away with leaving cold black tea for the Reverend Mr. Miller or his student, Hilary, when they are late for breakfast or tea, but when Miss Morris takes over the Parsonage as Mrs. Miller, her kind efficiency rescues Mr. Miller. The Parsonage has needed a mistress's hand.

In *Northbridge Rectory*, a true *comfort food* is Miss Pemberton's smoking-hot wartime dinner dish. A similar dish is called *pilaf* in both *The Headmistress* and *Miss Bunting*. One may associate it with the hypothetical *ragout* that Mr. Hurst, Mr. Bingley's brother-in-law, uses to test Elizabeth Bennet to determine whether she would prefer it to a plainer dish. Miss Pemberton's guests, accustomed to high standards but inured to the austerity of a third year of war, identify the ingredients admiringly, a discussion that previously would have been considered bad manners. Miss Pemberton, praised for her resourcefulness, is softened by that unaccustomed praise, and is immediately pressed by a guest, who in peace time was the representative of publisher Adrian Coates,[16] to write a book on wartime cooking.

Food also has an emotional significance unconnected with the chatelaines. During the war, the Beltons can no longer afford to keep up ancestral Harefield Park and must come down the hill to live in a smaller house on the main street (*TH*). On their first afternoon, Wheeler, the parlormaid, inexplicably puts six or seven delicate tea cups and saucers on the tea tray. Mr. and Mrs. Belton wonder why, until the three or four county families and neighbors arrive with two pots of peach jam, two rabbits and a basket of mushrooms, a cake made with real, hoarded flour, grapes, and a brace of partridges, and a bottle of whiskey. Thirkell has frequently emphasized the wartime restrictions on food, and she uses these generous gestures as a touchingly appropriate way of expressing sympathy and concern at a poignant moment.

Despite those war-time restrictions, the kitchens always do well, whatever the dining room may do. At Marling Hall at Christmastime, when older women on the estate come back to help out, "Tea flowed at all hours in spite of rationing, and somehow the whole kitchen had bacon for breakfast, though . . . the dining-room mostly did without" (*MH* 269), and at the Harveys' in the village, the housekeeper tells her helper, "You can have a cup of tea, Millie, and finish that bacon if you like" (*MH* 296).

Tea, with its concomitant buns, sliced "tin loaves," and heavy cake, is the inevitable accompaniment to church fetes, the Agricultural Show, and the annual meeting of the Barchester Archaeological Society. Thirkell comments, "The success of most learned societies is measured by their teas. The Barchester Archaeological had been accustomed to do its members very well" (*MB* 222,3), but six years of war have reduced the quality of the food. "But nothing has yet stopped people eating nasty cakes or drinking greedily cups of tea of an unknown and powdery brand flavored with artificial milk, and everyone was in very good humour . . . " (223).

For Thirkell, mealtimes afford primary occasions for meeting and socializing. In the Austen novels, balls—which frequently offer more privacy

—are where Elizabeth Bennet meets Mr. Darcy, where Catherine Morland and Henry Tilney are introduced, and where Mr. Knightley dances with Emma. The two authors are thus linked by the choreography of the dinner party and the dance. The carefully choreographed set-to of pairs at the dinner table and on the dance floor extends the metaphor of that society and reflects the unwritten law of the domestic comedy of manners: that one give one's undivided attention to one's immediate neighbor for an established length of time, and then bestow that attention on the other neighbor. Consider the scene in *Northanger Abbey* when Henry Tilney claims Catherine Morland's attention for the length of their dancing: "We have entered into a contract of mutual agreeableness for the space of an evening, and all our agreeableness belongs solely to each other for that time" (73). Further, Tilney likens a country-dance to the social contract of marriage.

Henry Tilney may be more teasing and facetious than Catherine always understands, but Alice Barton in *Pomfret Towers* resembles Catherine in her naiveté and her innate kind-heartedness, and the partnership of the dinner table resembles a dance. The weekend house party of that pre-war novel, its unstated purpose to find a suitable wife for the heir to Pomfret Towers, is carefully arranged according to those social conventions that order their lives and provide the security of ritual. The dinner on the Saturday evening not only reveals the commanding personality of the host but also lets Thirkell satirize the conventions:

> As the guests had not gone in in couples, there was the usual slight difficulty about setting to partners. Mrs. Rivers, halfway down the table, had annexed Professor Milward when the man on her other side had already begun talking to her. The mistake rapidly spread, and Alice found both her gentlemen had their heads turned to their other partner . . . Lord Pomfret, who noticed a great deal, had no intention of allowing the amenities of his table to be upset. 'Here, that's all wrong,' he said in a voice that stopped all conversation at his end of the table. 'Half of you talking to the wrong people. Hermione! *Hermione!* You talk to Mr. Cloves, and let Milward talk to Miss Faraday-Home. That's better.' (412)

Lord Pomfret then instructs Alice, who is in the running to become the future Countess of Pomfret and who is only shy, but not gauche, "You should never let that sort of thing happen . . . . It ruins any dinner" (412). From the point of view of social history, the reader of today is intrigued to find out how long a turn the partner would have: Benson says until about the time they had eaten their fish. Here Professor Milward and Miss Faraday - Home "fell into conversation about films which lasted through four courses" (*PT* 412).

The formal dinner party is only one part of the day where Thirkell's people meet. As daytime is woman's province, plans for the day are made or queried at breakfast, when everyone is present. In *Marling Hall* Mrs. Marling, having to manage a wartime household of farmer-husband, widowed daughter, unmarried younger daughter, unmarried younger son with an important wartime job, elderly governess making herself useful, reduced and sometimes unreliable staff, and, frequently, not enough vehicles or the petrol for them, asks, "What is everyone doing today?" Her daughter Lucy resents this question, but not until the whole family has appeared and been described by Thirkell's authorial voice. Lucy volunteers the information that a Captain Barclay "explodes bombs up the other side of Pook's Piece"; her father, a landowner, brings up an old association with Pook's Piece in which an upstart was prevented from buying into the neighborhood; and Miss Bunting, with her institutional memory of the aristocracy and nobility of Barsetshire, announces that a member of the Leslie family has been decorated in the news for doing something meritorious with a bomb. But Mrs. Marling sticks to the point, later finding out that Captain Barclay's "mother was a distant cousin of Lord Stoke and thus vaguely connected, though by no means related, to her husband's mother" (71). This connection attests to his suitability as a member of the family group.

"Whenever I see Lady Graham, I feel how entirely unnecessary intellect is in a woman." (TH 60)

One looks in vain for a "feminist" view in Thirkell's novels. Such an imposition of meaning would not fit her conservative, traditional view of women, although some of her heroines, of all ages, are spirited and independent. In *High Rising*, Laura Morland, her persona, says that she supports herself and her sons by writing novels, and she refuses two offers of marriage. Describing this novel, Margot Strickland, Thirkell's biographer, says, "The underlying impulse which holds it together comes from 'feminism,' but Mrs. Thirkell's women . . . would shrink from such a word . . . . The men are only satellites . . . nonetheless they may think themselves suns."[17] When Elsa Belton, who has an important wartime job, becomes engaged, her mother is "amused and touched to see Elsa the independent deferring to Captain Hornby's judgment and opinions" very prettily (*TH* 213). Elsa is more involved than her brothers in wanting to help save Harefield Park, but they are listened to by their father and she is regarded by her parents and brothers as unfeminine and interfering. Her parents apologize for Elsa, saying to her fiancé that "what she needs is a good beating" (287). In a neat psychological twist of illness as metaphor, Elsa then succumbs to the prevailing flu. One version of reality is that she has a difficult job, she is nervous, and it is hard to settle down to what her mother considers "normal." Dr. Perry gives a more traditional answer to Mrs. Belton: "Being in love plays the very deuce with these tough young women. Don't you let her play fast and loose with Captain Hornby. He's not a man to stand that sort of thing. Get her married whatever she says. She'll be all right with Hornby" (290).

The women are thus defined by their relationships with men. In the Austen novels this relationship is most frequently one of a father or father image: Emma Woodhouse as parent to her father, and Mr. Knightley as father figure to her; Elizabeth Bennet's sharing her father's sardonic point of view, and being protected by him from her mother's importunities regarding Mr. Collins; Fanny Price sheltered and fed by Sir Thomas but championed by her cousin Edmund during her younger years. The only true father and daughter relationship in the Thirkell novels is that of lower-class widower Sam Adams and his daughter, Heather.

In several of her novels Thirkell replaces the father with both a husband and a brother. Lydia Keith feels that she must see her brother Colin off to war after his embarkation leave despite the disapproval of her host, an old Army man, and the concern of her husband, Noel. Thirkell's authorial voice carefully points out that Noel, as an only child, "could not understand the peculiar link of brother and sister when the link is there" (*GU* 155).

We do find more of a supportive sisterhood between Jane Austen's Elinor and Marianne Dashwood and Jane and Elizabeth Bennet, although Eleanor Tilney does her best to stand friend to Catherine Morland. Probably the only true sister figure in the Thirkell novels is Lydia Keith Merton, who from their first meeting takes on a sister's role for war-shocked Leslie Waring, firmly watching out for her physical welfare and proving an ally in Leslie's romance with Philip Winter, despite the difficulties of communication posed by convention (*GU*).

The older heroines are feminine women whose husbands play a traditional male role. When the Belton family discusses the class system and the war, Elsa describes her co-workers as "clever" but not her sort. Her older brother, Freddy, a Commander in the navy, says, "When you're all doing things together everything shakes down; and when we're at sea we don't worry much about whom we'll meet on land," and their younger brother, Charles, in the army, contributes, "If you get awfully mucky and sweaty with a lot of fellows over your tanks, you find they're all right." Mrs. Belton then remarks, "If only life were one long crisis, everything would be perfect," and her husband's impatient response is, "But luckily it isn't. Don't talk nonsense, my dear" (*TH* 35).

Another example drawn from the three or four Harefield families features Mrs. Updike, wife of the solicitor, who "had more than once brought her very affectionate husband to the verge of shame by her kaleidoscopic view of life and her *obiter dicta* on the subject" (*TH* 303). Mrs. Watson, in charge of the camouflage at Hallbury, is also defined through her husband:

> Her husband's family had been known and respected in Hallbury for several generations and she was herself of good sub-county stock accustomed for generations to take responsibility and get things done . . . there was an unspoken feeling that her husband, who was extremely sensible, would be behind her and keep things in order. (*MB* 69)

A modern reader may be uncomfortable with these exchanges and the negative authorial comment, but Thirkell is portraying the roles and attitudes of women and men at the time—and the tradition she is comfortable with.

There are some socially disparate heroines whom Thirkell seems to admire wholeheartedly. In her early fifties, Mrs. Belton is brave in the face of genteel poverty, as the family, losing ground, is forced to give up its ancestral home. She finds herself always getting thinner and is momentarily wistful when she sees Lady Agnes Graham wearing the well-cut tweeds that she can no longer afford. Fortunately she does not have to contemplate her bedroom as being occupied by the somewhat unattractive students of the Hosiers' Girls' School now leasing Harefield Park. The Headmistress, Miss Sparling, another of Thirkell's favorites, has put Mrs. Belton's bedroom off limits. Mrs. Belton protects her husband, softening some of the radical changes in their way of life that the war has brought about. This protective trait is undoubtedly one of the strongest attributes of the older heroines. Mainly, however, she qualifies as heroine because she quietly exerts a civilizing influence on Sam Adams, whom Thirkell introduces in *The Headmistress*. She allows him to come into her home, as she would any other gentleman, although she has not been introduced to him. He is a hard-working, self-made man, a "rough diamond." She is strong in the face of an appalling reality: her class has been decimated by the war and displaced by the common man.

Miss Sparling, who *is* The Headmistress, is the best educated of Thirkell's heroines and is undeniably the most ladylike and acceptable of all her educated women. Because Harefield Park has been taken over by her school, the Beltons' well-being is tied to Miss Sparling's role as a neighbor and tenant, and they soon appreciate her common sense and good breeding. They are reassured further by the fact that the Vicar, Mr. Oriel, knew her grandfather, the importance of which is shown in Mrs. Belton's reaction:

> Miss Sparling at once went up in her estimation. It may be snobbishness to think the better of a person because your Vicar has known her grandfather who is a Canon; but it lies deep at the roots of social life, and there is good reason for it. (*TH* 140)

Early in their acquaintance Mr. Carton, an Oxford don who lives in Harefield, describes Miss Sparling with the highest masculine accolade: "A person who, if of the opposite sex, would not be amiss in a common-room" (*TH* 164). His antipathy towards female dons changes to admiration for her scholarship and her self-effacing modesty, as well as her demeanor of discreet approachability to her students. This picture of Miss Sparling as a scholar who is also feminine is in direct contrast with Thirkell's portrayals of the shortcomings of university women, particularly her counterpart, Miss Pettinger, principal of the Barsetshire Girls' High School. Thirkell is not emphasizing a class distinction here, as she is with Sam Adams, but a professional one, demonstrated not only by attitude—"Miss Pettinger . . . held the mistaken belief that when off duty she was almost as others, though better educated and more important" (*SH* 264)—and words, but by clothing. We see the contrast through Miss Sparling's eyes on Bobbin Day at Harefield School:

> (Miss Pettinger) was wearing a kind of Robin Hood hat of green felt with one long brown quill stuck jauntily through the high crown (and) a rather meagre piece of brown veiling . . . . (Miss Sparling) knew that she, Miss Sparling, a

member of a great City Company, was dressed exactly as in her position she should be dressed, even down to the V opening and the piece of lace. (*TH* 230)

When war breaks out, Lydia Keith, Thirkell's favorite young heroine, although a natural swashbuckler, remains at home. Lydia approaches running the estate as the at-home "son" while her brothers are away fighting or carrying on the family law firm. She also wrests the reins of the household from her tired mother, assuming responsibility for the evacuée children and teachers billeted on the family, and taking her turn in the community kitchen with lunch for the evacuées, all despite her longing to be in the thick of the struggle on the home front. Later in the war, even though she has married, she wants to be a Land Girl to be closer to the war effort.

Lydia is a Thirkell heroine who has known her heroes, her brother Colin and Noel Merton, during her formative years. Characterized as an Amazon, Lydia, "still in her revolting school uniform, carries off the much-sought-after barrister (Noel) a captive of her bow and spear" (*CBI* 468). We know the state of her heart, for at Rose Birkett's wedding on the eve of the war, the "old" Lydia has said to Noel, "'I'm glad it wasn't me . . . I mean all this marrying business,' . . . only if Noel wanted to marry anyone he had better not tell her till afterwards, as she was sure it would be someone ghastly that she'd absolutely loathe" (*CBI* 431)—because she would loathe anyone who took her place with Noel, the one person besides Colin whom she lives to please.

Her mother's increasing ill health and her own spiralling burdens, not the least of which is loneliness, give Lydia, strong-minded and self-sufficient until now, as well as innocent, the ability to acknowledge her own need for someone to depend on. Therefore, when the news of her father's death brings Noel home and they discuss friends' postponing marriage until after the war, Lydia confesses to him, "'If I loved anyone I'd marry them at once.' Then to Noel's intense surprise her face went bright pink and she looked at him as if imploring forgiveness" (591). She is going against Henry

Tilney's warning: "in both (matrimony and dancing), man has the advantage of choice, woman only the power of refusal . . . " (*NA* 73).

Loneliness defines another young Thirkell heroine. Jane Gresham, whose naval husband has been missing in the Pacific for four and one-half years, lives with her father and eight-year-old son. Like Lydia, she would like to lose herself in a war job but accepts her domestic responsibilities. Into this wartime isolation comes Mr. Adams and a brief summertime encounter with strong undercurrents of attraction, longing, comfort, and help given and received. The war has undermined Jane's accepted sense of self and class: "She knew that she was more and more aware of his personality and was letting herself be attracted by it . . . but every subject led her exhausted mind back to Mr. Adams who was not a gentleman and never would be" (*MB* 245); Mr. Adams's "tweed-clad bulk beside her seemed safe and comforting" (252); and

> hope deferred was wearing her down, and to fall into those large arms and forget everything forever would be a relief past words. At the same time another Jane knew that this was not only weakness but quite silly . . . . (253)

However, subverting Jane's belief of his not being a gentleman—a rationale traditionally adopted by her class, because it provides useful stiffening against her physical attraction to him—is the reality of the force he represents and the new network of the middle class, which he epitomizes. Through what he calls his "pals" in Intelligence, Mr. Adams is able to learn the whereabouts of Jane's husband, Francis, just as he has succeeded in placing Jane's father on the board of directors of his Hogglestock rolling mills. Earlier, when befriended by the Beltons, he uses his influence to get the war agricultural commission to call off its misguided threat to put a non-arable piece of Mr. Belton's land into cultivation. He must now be dealt with as an undeniable power, no matter how socially inappropriate his stream-of-consciousness speech, his loud clothing, and his commanding personality.

Neither wife nor widow, Jane lets her guard down. For his part, aware of society's rules and regulations, Mr. Adams knows that it is ungentlemanly to be involved with someone else's wife and uses every channel to learn whether Francis has survived. In what is their last meeting, he precedes his reassuring bulletin with this embarrassing statement: "What I'm going to say has nothing to do with anything concerning any ideas you may have had or I may have had about any feelings that may have passed in a temporary sort of way between you and I" (309). While he is telling her this, Thirkell describes, in a masterful bit of writing, what Jane, "her cheeks burning," sees:

> a spider who was sitting in his autumn net, waiting for the tradesmen to call . . . . The spider, sitting comfortably in his study, smoking and reading the Daily Arachnoid, felt his back-door thread quiver. He put down his pipe and paper and went gently down the passage. Jane went as white as she had been red. She tried to say something, but no sound came from her and the spider held her whole attention. He had by now ascertained that it was the butcher and was going cautiously to the back-door to meet him . . . . The spider, having removed his shoes and tiptoed to the back-door, had tied the butcher up in a neat parcel, put him in the larder, and returned to the study, where he picked up his pipe and went on reading a review of 'An eight-legged Traveller in English Hedgerows,' by Webly Spinner. Jane stared and stared at him and said nothing. (309, 310)

In short, Mr. Adams is a foil for this other class of people; he tests their mettle. It is interesting to note that, unlike Jane Austen's Mr. Collins, who also is a barbarian at the gates but who is self-serving, Mr. Adams does the right thing time after time, and the reader is attracted to him.

"All the world not only loves a lover, but feels itself entitled to overlook and discuss every movement of these marked beings." (TH 265)

One of the strongest affinities with the Austen novels is the ubiquitous subject of courtship in the community, at a time when women are defined by the men they are with or aspire to marry. Charlotte Lucas is estranged, at least for a time, from Elizabeth Bennet, her dearest friend, because she is willing to accept as her mate Mr. Collins, a man whom she does not love and cannot respect, rather than remain an old maid. Consider the united efforts helping Henry Crawford plead his suit to Fanny Price, including the importunities of his sister, Mary. Mary thinks that Fanny should be triumphant for having won a man who has caused such heartburning among London mamas and daughters. Sir Thomas reminds Fanny of Mr. Crawford's influence and efforts on her sailor brother William's behalf and the possible advantages of the match to her other brothers and sisters. He confesses that he would have been glad to have Julia or Maria sought in marriage by Mr. Crawford. Lady Bertram gives unaccustomed advice: she not only thinks better of Fanny for having been the object of this proposal, but tells her that it is her duty to accept such an offer. More vicious is Aunt Norris's resentment, based as it is on Mr. Crawford's preference for Fanny over her favorites, Julia or Maria. Worst of all is the lack of empathy from her beloved cousin, Edmund, who has an interest in Henry's sister. All of these reactions reveal and satirize the separate, subjective interests of the speakers.

More humorous is the community's preoccupation with the Bennet daughters' prospects. The apparent resumption of Mr. Bingley's courtship of Jane, that has been conducted very much in public, causes neighbor Mrs. Long to say, "Ah! Mrs. Bennet, we shall have her at Netherfield at last" (*P&P* 342). When Mr. Bingley ultimately rewards these expectations, "The Bennets were speedily pronounced to be the luckiest family in the world, though only a few weeks before, when Lydia had first run away, they had been generally proved to be marked out for misfortune" (350).

We know enough about the heroines to be convinced, as Jane Austen intends us to be, that the couples will be sincerely happy after marriage, despite having to encounter, for example, Mrs. Elton's ill-natured comments regarding Emma and Mr. Knightley's domestic arrangements.

From top to bottom, Thirkell's communities are vicariously and happily concerned in the local courtships. Lord Pomfret bets his wife a dozen pairs of gloves that Mr. Foster will propose to Sally Wicklow, not Alice Barton (*PT* 274). The servants also have a contributing role in the courtships. Gudgeon, the butler at Rushwater, comes upon John Leslie and Mary Preston embracing in the main hall, and suddenly his personality expands: he "was for once taken aback by what he saw, and uttered an exclamation." John Leslie tells him "It's all right": Miss Preston and he are engaged. Gudgeon replies, "I am very happy to hear it, sir. If I may say so, Mr. John, nothing could give more satisfaction in the Room and the Hall" and he "executed a nuptial fanfare" upon the mealtime gong (*WS* 264). Peters, the butler at Pomfret Towers, "almost hastened to overtake Mr. Foster. 'May I presume, sir,' he said, 'to offer my very respectful congratulations?'" Upon being asked by Mr. Foster how he knows, Peters says, "pityingly, 'One generally does, sir. Miss Wicklow, sir, is highly thought of in the Room, also in the Hall if I may presume to mention it'" (*PT* 277). Even Spencer, the butler at Staple Park, when castigated royally by Daphne for mailing Lady Bond's letters too early, reacts in keeping:

> Of course under any other circumstances Spencer would have given notice on the spot, but Something . . . told him that something was up between Miss Stoner and Mr. Bond and under these peculiar circumstances he felt he had better leave things be. To everyone's intense surprise he said, 'I'm very sorry, my lady, very sorry indeed, miss. It shall never occur again . . . .'(*BL* 297)

The female servants know what is going on because Cook reads tea leaves: Hilda, who cooks and keeps house for Frances and Geoffrey Harvey, says she "saw it all in the tea-cup, first night we was here," that she and the Marling estate carpenter, Mr. Govern, would be married (*MH* 297); and Cook in *Growing Up* sees a disfigured stranger in her cup, who turns out to be one-armed Tommy Needham, back from the war to marry Octavia Crawley as soon as he has a living (299).

The community's interest is ardent. With the Beltons now in the village, the neighbors can follow the progress of Captain Hornby's courtship of Elsa Belton, even keeping track of their whereabouts. After general surmising,

Mrs. Hoare, with decent archness, said she had seen them from her back window going across the park. Everyone said 'Ah' in a very knowing way, so true it is that all the world not only loves a lover, but feels itself entitled to overlook and discuss every movement of these marked beings. (*TH* 264,5)

When Lydia Keith is waiting for Noel to return, her longing can be inferred from an exchange between Mrs. Bissell and her wartime neighbors, Miss Hampton and Miss Bent, all of them versed in psychology:

> 'There goes Lydia Keith,' said Miss Hampton. 'Nice girl. She looks thin lately. Wonder if anything's wrong.'
> 'Miss Keith is a very peculiar and I might say almost abnormal type,' said Mrs. Bissell.
> 'How?' said Miss Bent . . .
> 'She is perfectly normal,' said Mrs. Bissell. (*CBI* 572)

—normal, that is, within what we now term a male-oriented, patriarchal society, for a young woman who is disadvantaged by attitudes that will not permit her to express her loneliness.

Miss Phipps of the Post Office, who has just allowed Daphne to extract Lady Bond's letters from the mail bag, "guided by a Something, followed (Daphne) to the door and looked out. What she saw (Daphne in the car with C.W. Bond) evidently satisfied her, for she remarked aloud to herself, 'And a very nice young ladyship too'" (*BL* 299).

The concept of marriage as happy ending, or sole answer, reflects society's position towards women of this class with little change since the time of Jane Austen. Reviewer Louise Field's dictum on *Pomfret Towers*, that "Each and every one (of the love affairs) might well be labeled 'Object, matrimony,'"[17] applies to all Thirkell's novels. At first some of Thirkell's heroines—Lydia Keith, Sally Wicklow, Daphne Stoner, and Lucy Marling—give the impression of being just off the hockey field and are hardly aware of men as men. Propinquity, not flirtatiousness, works for them. Sally Wicklow is "a martinet in the field or the kennels" and appears to think more highly of dogs and horses than of men. Her grasp of the estate work is as good as either her brother Roddy's, the estate agent for Lord

Pomfret, or Mr. Foster's, the future heir. After they have spent an afternoon straightening out the agent's office, the latter proposes. She reacts "with a kind of yelp, as every one of her manly standards went down . . . and gulped and sobbed on his shoulder as she would have scorned to do even for the death of a dog" (*PT* 479). *Yelp* is a doggy term, *manly standards* speaks for itself, and *gulped* and *sobbed* can only be seen as delivering oneself into the victor's hands.

Thirkell associates other young woman with dogs: George Knox's daughter, Sybil, tries to write to please her father (*HR*), but she is embarrassingly devoid of talent; she breeds dogs. When her father has the flu, Sybil says that he is being kept shut up as though he had distemper. At the end of *Pomfret Towers*, delicate, timid Alice Barton is told by Sally Wicklow's brother, Roddy, that if she would like to walk some puppies at the kennel in the summer, he will give her a hand. As Henry Tilney says, ". . . a teachableness of disposition in a young lady is a great blessing" (*NA* 112), and Alice accordingly qualifies for the protection and care of a man who "almost enveloped (her) with his great height and breadth and his loose shabby tweeds, but Alice found it comfortable and reassuring" (*PT* 341).

During the houseparty weekend at Pomfret Towers, Lady Pomfret has favored Alice Barton as future wife of the heir because of the family connection: Mrs. Barton is her long-time friend, and at one time Lady Pomfret hoped that Mrs. Barton and her son might become more than good friends. She finds that Alice paints, an activity that would be completely suitable for a Countess; her own mother-in-law had "a remarkable talent for watercolour drawings." But Lord Pomfret knows better: "She'd never do. She's a nice girl, but she's a delicate girl . . . what he wants is a wife with plenty of good health and good sense, someone who will look after the place" (*PT* 481), and proposes Sally Wicklow.

Another heroine with good health and good sense is Daphne Stoner, who offers herself to Lady Bond as secretary. She neatly bests Spencer, the

Stonor and for penniless Mary Preston (WS). For hearty, self-sufficient heroines like Sally Wicklow, Lydia Keith, and Delia Brandon, who is immature enough to carve Hilary Grant's name on the gardener's best marrow, as well as for painfully shy Alice Barlow, who is reluctant to leave the safety of home, there is also the analogy of the ugly duckling becoming a swan, or even a sleeping beauty awakened by a kiss from the prince.

In these significant romances the appropriateness of the future mistress of the estate is as important as love or compatibility. Lady Bond has to be brought round to accept Daphne, less because Daphne has been acting as her secretary than because of "her natural tendency to disapprove of everything which she had not originated herself" (BL 292). This attitude is different in degree from Lady Catherine de Bourgh's insulting remark to Elizabeth Bennet: "Are the shades of Pemberley to be thus polluted?" (P&P 357). Lady Bond acquiesces, however, when Daphne saves face for her by vanquishing the butler and then using guile to retrieve her employer's important letters from the post office. Marrying upward is a matter for both conflict and comedy!

Clearly, there is an economic as well as social factor to these alliances: the young men will inherit money and land, as well as a title, so the future of the family line is at stake. Gillie Foster's proposal to Sally Wicklow, with her initial reaction of surprised resistance, and an undertone of overcoming the barriers of an independent, competent young woman in the face of a suitable match, is down-to-earth: he says that his Uncle Giles, Lord Pomfret, will be pleased, and he is. Also balanced and suitable is the engagement of Elsa Belton, who listens eagerly to what Captain Hornby says about the family place in Scotland, because "coming as she did of a landowning family whose daughters were brought up to marry into other landowning families and strike root firmly in new soil, the prospect sounded inviting to her" (TH 194). When prosperous Laurence Dean becomes engaged to penniless Margaret Tebben, his aunt Mrs. Palmer is more outspoken: "I would have

butler, in favor of Lord Bond over the rightful possession of the key to the piano. When she tells Lord Bond the whereabouts of a treasured bibelot he has been looking for, he says, "Good girl. You know the place better than I do," so that when C.W. Bond tells his father that he and Daphne are engaged, landowner Lord Bond's priorities are reflected in his response: "And on the Agricultural night too. Well, I couldn't be more pleased if I'd got every first prize at the Show. She's a treasure, C.W. A girl that can get the better of Spencer will do anything" (*BL* 284). County magistrate Lord Pomfret also shows the influence of the landowners' priorities on courtship when he arrives on the scene and is told of the engagement: "Young man like you coming into a nice little place, can't get engaged too soon. Keep you steady" (293), a timeless application of Jane Austen's immortal words, "It is a truth universally acknowledged, that a single man in possession of a good fortune must be in want of a wife (*P&P* 3). When congratulating Daphne he finds that her father was in the same regiment as his own son, so a relative nobody, but one who can lay her hands on elusive *objets d'art* and put Spencer in his place, as well as knowing the name and responsibilities of every person on the estate, is now established as being a worthy partner for the heir of Staple Park.

With their happy endings, these comedy of manners romances have a fairy-tale quality. In a fairy-tale, almost Gothic, situation, Margaret Tebben is a fair maiden "rescued" by Lawrence Dean. Mr. Tebben

> was enchanted by (his) pretty, sweet-tempered daughter . . . he hadn't been able to send Margaret to a University, nor did he think she was the type of girl to benefit by it, but . . . what was going to become of her? (*AF* 86).

Her mother, although not unfond of Margaret, is a poor manager and does not want an Angel in the House. Margaret has no money for new clothes and, like Jane Fairfax, is wondering how to enter the "slave trade." Lawrence says, not very helpfully, "I'd hate you to have a job . . . promise me you never will" (146). Marriage is the answer for her, as it is for Daphne liked Laurence to marry well . . . this place will be his, and we must want to see him with the right sort of wife" (*AF* 159). Again it is the husband who is realistic and reassuring: "Margaret would be a very good wife . . . . It's time Laurence settled down. He must have children . . . . He doesn't need money" (159).

How significant is it that Lady Catherine de Bourgh does not have a husband, as the Thirkell chatelaines do, to ease her down from her untenable position on Elizabeth Bennet? Other, heavier obstacles are in Elizabeth's way, with Lady Catherine not the only one representing the obstacle of community disapproval, and Darcy himself presenting others. Elizabeth's development is a psychological reversal, that of being ready to be a full partner in running Pemberley, which she has been too prejudiced to contemplate. The situations of Thirkell's young heroines are socially and economically analogous to that of Elizabeth: they are of the same social class, all gentry, and Sally Wicklow's brother is the under-estate agent for the Pomfrets, but neither Daphne Stonor nor Margaret Tebben is well off financially. A social consideration is voiced by Lady Pomfret when she prefers Alice Barton and a different one by Lady Bond when she is slow to accept Daphne.

In the Thirkell novels, the reader becomes as involved with the young heroines as the community does, but then is concerned that their individual voices are no longer heard. What happens to Alice Barton after she has gone through the rite of passage of the Pomfret Towers house party and seems assured of the protection of stalwart Roddy Wicklow? We meet her again at a wartime Red Cross meeting at the Deanery, when Lydia Keith identifies her: "young Mrs. Roddy Wicklow," but she is described only as with "large dark timid eyes" (*CBI* 130), which sounds representative enough, but not otherwise revealing. As Countess of Pomfret, the former Sally Wicklow stops raising dogs and raises her own three children, and serves on every county committee. Although that is not "subsiding into contented domesticity,"[18] her unmarried cousin Lucy Marling's opinion is that Sally was "much more sensible when she was running the beagles. Now she's got Gillie and the children to look after she seems much less interesting" (*MH* 275).

We find an equally consuming community interest in the future of Miss Morris, one of Thirkell's older heroines, who has been companion to a succession of devouring old ladies, the latest of whom, a Brandon relative, has just died. Lady Norton's patronizing suggestion to her recalls Mrs. Elton's lecturing Jane Fairfax about the advantages of being a governess and, although better meant, is preposterous: "My eldest niece, the one who lives in Cape Town, is needing a secretary. She does an enormous amount of work among diseased half-castes and writes to me that life is most interesting. She cannot offer a salary, but the opportunities are unlimited" (*TB* 276). In the end the Reverend Mr. Miller gains a true partner in Miss Morris, his old love, and she a selfless husband. At the same time she is rescued from a bleak future of repression and subservience and returned to where she belongs and triumphs: running a parish.

Miss Morris is one of the heroines for whom Thirkell makes a suitable match by removing her from the seclusion her job demands to visit the kind relatives of the most recent old lady. Jane Austen has Mr. Knightley and Mrs. Weston agree that for Emma, in similar seclusion with her valetudinarian father, there is no one of her class in Highbury for her to meet and who would "attach" her, and Emma is unlikely to go elsewhere to meet someone. This is not like some of Austen's heroines, particularly Catherine Morland, who is invited to accompany a generous neighbor to Bath where she meets a most eligible young clergyman (*NA*).

"A good many people of their age still looked on the war work of the younger generation as a kind of amiable hobby." (GU 123)

For Thirkell's similarly placed heroines—and they are similarly placed, because these comedy of manners novels are set in the country—the war provides the requisite opportunity "to go elsewhere." The young women can now get away from the small circle of the three or four families in a country village, which not only improves their prospects of marriage, but also broadens their experiences and understanding. Some meet military men on leave or stationed near them before being sent overseas, as does Leslie Waring, niece of landowner Sir Harry Waring, of Beliers Priory. She is at the Priory on leave from her important wartime job in London to recover from a breakdown when she meets Philip Winter, stationed at the nearby camp. She, as a landowner's niece and with the responsibilities of her class, sees in her job the wider implications for women, and she comments apprehensively to her aunt, "Most of the women I had under me were incredibly efficient . . . . But it's all upside down. It is quite horrid not to be able to feel that men are superior beings," and because these are two women speaking, Leslie's words seem to reflect Thirkell's romanticized view of men rather than satirize it. "Most of the women in my department don't want to settle down. They want to go on living with lots of other women . . . and having all their fun in crowds . . . . They really like cocoa suppers in the dormitory" (*GU* 117).

For another group of young women, the war has meant a step up in the world. But this mixing of the classes causes uneasiness in those who are nominally their superiors. This is the point of view of Oliver Marling:

> Nice, hard-working and conscientious as the secretaries and typists were, he could not talk to them easily. Cinemas, the rationing of cosmetics . . . appeared to be the limit of their conversational powers. They were quick, intelligent, obedient, ready to stay overtime whenever wanted, and Oliver marvelled . . . at the gulf which was set between himself and his friends and what were at the present moment the actual pillars, if not the saviours of society. (*MH* 143)

For Elsa Belton, also, there is some bewilderment:

> Some of the girls at my job are real ladies. I mean, like me if I am a lady, but

the rest aren't. I mean they are awfully clever and good-looking and say the right things, but somehow they aren't just right. And all their people seem quite rich, but I don't think they'd fit in at Harefield. (*TH* 34)

Her mother, that much older, is equally wistful, knowing that if the times were normal, Elsa would not be mixing with the girls who have brains but no background. Yet Mrs. Belton is the one who becomes a surrogate mother to Heather Adams and quiet mentor to her father, Sam Adams, an unwelcome outsider but an undeniable force in the Brave New World.

In Thirkell's popular wartime novel, *Northbridge Rectory*, middle-class England comes into its own; its retired naval officers and widows and unmarried women—always women—to all intents and purposes run the war on the home front. They, like their younger counterparts Leslie Waring and Elsa Belton of a different class, can now show initiative, drive, organizing ability, and authority, qualities that haven't been in demand since World War I.

Such war-time challenges to women have no real counterpart in the Austen novels. There was no home war effort or rationing as in World War II, as Thirkell describes, nor any war work for women, as in both world wars. Thirkell's character Mr. Birkett, Headmaster of Southbridge School, voices what readers generally have accepted: that "during the Napoleonic wars . . . Miss Austen was able totally to ignore current events" because "communications were slow" (*MB* 198), although in *Pride and Prejudice* the militia is in Meryton and then Brighton, where it would not be without the ongoing war, providing a Wickham for Lydia Bennet to run away with. In *Persuasion* Captain Wentworth makes his fortune from a form of piracy in the aftermath of the war. That fortune renders him acceptable to Anne Elliot's father and sister as Anne's suitor. She thereby enters a new life as a naval officer's wife. While her status is on a different social level from that of a landowner's daughter, Anne can share the responsibility for her husband's charges, just as she was the one to carry out the duties of the family at Kellynch. By contrast, in terms of position in society, Fanny and the other young Jane Austen heroines become eligible, through strength of character and understanding of self, to be equal partners with their landowner husbands, captured in Jane Austen's description of Marianne Dashwood's future social position: "entering on new duties, placed in a new home, a wife, the mistress of a family (the people on the estate), and the patroness of a village" (*S&S* 379).

"That's all right," said Captain Fairweather, giving (Geraldine) a hearty hug with his left arm. "We'll probably get married, come the peace . . . ." (*CBI* 271)

The constraints, the formality, the implications of *touch* by these comedy of manners writers make the demonstrations of affection and expressions of intent in Thirkell's novels far closer to those of the Austen novels than to those countenanced at the close of the twentieth century. Frank Churchill puts Jane Fairfax in danger of exposure and censure for their secret engagement by publicly asking a question that inadvertently reveals particular knowledge of what is going on in Highbury, information that could have come only from a local correspondent, and of which his usual correspondent, his stepmother, Mrs. Weston, denies all knowledge. Jane Austen also offers two completely sincere expressions of feeling in extreme moments. Darcy's "serious, parting, look" (*P&P* 279) is tantamount to a kiss, their social relationship having entered an entirely new and promising stage when Elizabeth visits Pemberley, but she has now been summoned back to Longbourn following Lydia's elopement. Again, when Frank Churchill's engagement to Jane Fairfax is revealed and Mr. Knightley thinks Emma has been made unhappy, she finds "her arm drawn within his, and pressed against his heart" (*E* 425).

Little has changed regarding appearances and demonstrations of affection in these writers following in the Jane Austen tradition. The modern reader may find it amusing that Delafield's Barbara Blenkinsop asks the

Provincial Lady "if I think a girl makes herself cheap by allowing a man friend to take her out to dinner in Soho?" but the Provincial Lady's immediate reaction is to visualize her small daughter Vicky in taffeta as bridesmaid (*DPL* 119). Thirkell's Daphne Stonor, before the misunderstanding with C. W. Bond is straightened out, suddenly finds herself engaged to Alister Cameron because she has cried on his shoulder. Both Kate Keith and Mary Preston are flustered and distressed to realize that they have each been seen by their true loves with someone else's gallant arm around them. In fact, the true loves do infer something serious—the intention of marriage—from those fleeting passages.

Elbows seem to have a special quality. When Elsa Belton and Captain Hornby lean on the parapet of Arcot House,

> Their elbows touched. And though Elsa felt no particular emotion at this contact, a vague unformed filament of thoughts, drifting like mist across her mind, informed her that Captain Hornby's elbow, even separated from her by a shirt and heavy blue coat (his) and a woollen pullover and cardigan (hers), had about it something which separated it from the elbows of other men, exquisite, apart. (*TH* 125)

A similar gently mocking moment occurs in *Summer Half* when Everard Carter and Kate Keith share a hymnal:

> if he took the book he would have to touch her, and . . . if he did touch her he thought he might go mad, and as he was right at the end of the pew furthest from the door, that would have been uncomfortable for everyone . . . both had ample leisure to reflect upon the astounding beauty of emotion as roused by the involuntary contact of elbows. (*SH* 258, 9).

The traditional reticence reflects Thirkell's single standard of appropriate behavior for women; the warmest word she allows her heroines to use to describe how they feel about the heroes is "comfortable."

August Folly, and no doubt this is the reason for its name, contains three romances, two of them traditional in their revealing language and suggestive atmosphere. Laurence Dean is a manly fellow and, with the backdrop of the Greek drama the village is putting on, Margaret, dressed in her Phaedra

robes, looks at him and thinks, "How is it possible that Phaedra should not
have been consumed by her desire for Hippolytus?" (153). He then *falls*.
They are the earliest pair in the Thirkell novels to have language associated
with them that implies sexual tension; only ten years later does Thirkell
create another suggestive situation, for Jane Gresham and Mr. Adams.
When Margaret is induced to visit Laurence after the fall results in a
sprained ankle, and she puts her head on his shoulder, a Dean sister who
sees them says, "I suppose you're engaged." More important in the comedy
of manners is that a maid then walks past, shrieks—and Margaret is
"compromised."

The last romantic interest in the novel, Mrs. Dean, is sensuous and
passive, and her becoming white or green draperies and the velvet summer
nights affect young Richard Tebben so that he writes poetry about her.

Thirkell's novels offer no illicit liaisons, no breaking up of a marriage;
in short, none of the complications of plot customary in Jane Austen's time.
We find no Willoughby to ruin Eliza Brandon and treat Marianne Dashwood
cavalierly; no Wickham to try to seduce Georgianna Darcy and succeed with
Lydia Bennet; no Henry Crawford and Maria Bertram to flout the decorum
of society. An empathetic Mr. Dean rescues his wife from the tedium of
Richard's attention with the sly betrayal that she is close to fifty. In *Before
Lunch*, Catherine Middleton, a reticent woman in her forties, married to a
well-established architect and gentleman farmer who is a compulsive talker,
becomes involved, wordlessly and painfully, with Denis Stonor, her sickly
neighbor who is probably fifteen years younger. This is an impossible
situation for the comedy of manners, and there is no question of fulfillment.
Thirkell provides an immediate and legitimate departure to New York and
the world of music for Denis, and a continuing controlled life for Catherine.

"(Dr. Perry) was fond of his pastor though with no very high opinion of his worldly wisdom." (TH 16)

The clergy traditionally has enjoyed a role in the comedy of manners. Three of Jane Austen's clergymen are the social equals, if not the social superiors, of the heroines and are the ones whom the heroines marry: Henry Tilney, Edmund Bertram, and Edward Ferrars. Jane Austen has even said that the subject of *Mansfield Park* is *ordination* (*L* 76 298). The other two, Mr. Collins and Mr. Elton, exhibit misguided social pretensions in proposing to the heroines, but are rebuffed. Even those two, however, must continue to be dealt with: Mr. Collins as a relative and then later as Charlotte Lucas's husband is an inescapable member of Elizabeth Bennet's circle until she removes to Pemberley; and Mr. Elton is the Highbury clergyman who presides at Emma and Mr. Knightley's marriage.

Over a century later, although fewer well-educated second sons have chosen the church as a career, each of the Thirkell novels has a clergyman as an integral part of the community. They are no longer the obvious choice of the heroine, but they have other roles. The touchstone of their acceptability to the higher clergy, to the one bestowing the living, and to the community, is the soundness of their views on the incumbent Bishop, "less for the job than for the social aspects," as critic Patricia Spacks points out.[19] The chatelaines regard church-going as a pre-ordained Sunday activity, a gentle opportunity for Thirkell to mock the clergy. Mrs. Middleton hopes her new neighbors will accompany her to church: ". . . one must go or there would be no one in the Laverings pew . . . . It is so nice if one can make a good show for the Rector" (*BL* 73); and Lady Emily Leslie says, "It is disappointing" that some of the family won't be staying for communion, "because the Vicar does dearly love a good house . . . " (*WS* 7). Mr. Moxon comes in for more mockery than any of his brethren: he scents possibilities for fellowship, "inspires a violent and well grounded dislike at sight," and moves Mr. Fanshawe to pronounce, "I do not know why young men who selflessly devote their time and energy and in many cases their means, to that very noble task of organizing and helping boys less happily placed than themselves, should almost invariably be conceited bores" (*AF* 117). The Reverend Mr. Miller, one of Thirkell's clergymen who marry a heroine, is subjected to such comments from Mrs. Brandon, his patroness, as "It is a *rag*, one couldn't wear that frock even in church. You know what I mean, don't you, Mr. Miller?" (*TB* 186). He repeats his words—"Indeed, indeed"—and the younger Brandons wonder how he will dress for dinner, failing "the cassock and biretta that were the joy of his life" (*TB* 21).

During the war, clergymen are some of the few males left in the community. One of these is Father Fewling, and although Mrs. Villars in Northbridge does not count him or her husband, the Rector, as men for any social gathering, "Tubby" Fewling must appeal to her for protection from the ubiquitous unmarried churchgoing ladies of the parish. Tommy Needham loses his right arm while a chaplain on the North African front, then returns to the Dean's daughter and an opportune living, his views on the Bishop reflecting those of his patron, Sir Harry Waring, as well as those of his future father-in-law.

The local priest who deserves most credit for forbearance is Mr. Bannister (*WS*), whose church is supported by the Leslies, Thirkell's first and probable favorite of her original three or four families. As she has done for years, Lady Emily comes late to the Sunday morning service and so disrupts with her "intromissions" that Mr. Bannister is nerving himself to say something to her when, in 1918, the news of her eldest son's death stops any thought of chiding.

Do we take for granted that comedy of manners novels reflect social history? The Leslies' son was not the only one killed in 1918; so was young George Waring, son of Sir Harry and Lady Waring (*GU*). Lord and Lady Pomfret's only son, Mellings, was killed in a border skirmish in India (*PT*). Few of the families are untouched by World War II: Lettice Watson's husband is drowned at Dunkirk (*MH*); then-Lieutenant Freddy Belton's Wren sweetheart is killed in an air-raid early in the war (*TH*); Robin Dale has lost a foot at Anzio and Tommy Needham an arm in North Africa; Jane Gresham's sailor husband has been missing in the Pacific for four and one-half years.

"(Alice Barton) wrote a handsome Collins to Lady Pomfret." (*PT* 216)

When Thirkell's son describes her as *snobbish*, he means that her subject is the landed gentry's privileged way of life until the war in 1939 changed that world. But this world is where Thirkell is most comfortable—even though she laughs at its inhabitants. If Thirkell is a snob, she is a snob about language. In the comedy of manners, language and speech patterns reveal social class and degree of education and culture. Earlier, in the Austen novels, the only characters who speak differently, betraying their lack of education as well as refinement, are Lucy Steele, when she lapses, and her sister Anne: "La!" "monstrous happy," "an't she," "had went away," "rid into the country," "how was they to live on that" (*SS* 273). None of the important characters in the Benson or Delafield novels show their origins in that way.

Since Thirkell's time, "between you and I" has, inexplicably and deplorably, become established usage almost world-wide. It can no longer be assumed that the reader of *The Headmistress* will grasp, as Thirkell intends, that Mr. Adams is revealing his social status by his misuse of grammar and accepted pronunciation and his catchwords: "ever since Mrs. Adams left Heth and I," "me and Heth thought," "the invite," "seckertary," "instink," "idear," "arst," "Timon Tide . . . " and his favorite third-person pronouncement, "Sam Adams's word is as good as his bond." He also talks too much, in the opinion of the reticent upper classes: "Mrs. Belton had a firm conviction that Mr. Adams, even if he didn't stay the night, was going to talk for at least two hours without stopping" (*TH* 284).

Some of the young heroines also betray themselves when they speak. Rose Birkett (*SH*) is acknowledged as beautiful, but her vocabulary is strictly limited: "sickening" and, alternately, "wonderful" are her catchwords one year, and "foully dispiriting" the next.   Rose is the daughter of a schoolmaster and has been to a "good" school, Barchester Girls' High. Its principal, Miss Pettinger, promotes curtseying and Latin odes, but few of the products of that establishment reflect a high degree of literacy.   Lucy Marling, also one of the products, is known for her trite phrase, "I'll tell you what."   Another, Mrs. Turner's niece Betty (*NR*) whose last name is forever unknown, is identified by the catchword "ackcherly."[20]   The speech of Mr. Bissell, headmaster of the Hosiers' Boys' School, a lower echelon school billeted on Southbridge Boys' School in the early years of the war, is satirized, both for the malapropisms— "Panderer" for "Pandora"—and those telltale pronouns: "It was a great grief to Mrs. Bissell and he that they had no chicks" (*CBI* 64); "but we talked it over, her and I, and I'm sure she feels like I do" (71); "to stay at the Carters' house would give very great pleasure to Mrs. Bissell and he" (76); and "the world has deteriated of late, and it's up to we schoolmasters to make it a better place for the boys" (93). His better educated hearers are too well-bred to show any surprise, but they are conscious of their adjustments to common usage: "With a sudden inspiration (Everard Carter) told Mr. Bissell that he reciprocated his sentiments" (93), meaning that he is pandering to Mr. Bissell's frame of reference.

Thirkell has an equally masterful hand with the incongruities that make humor: "the small home farm, which has been for generations a source of great pride, pleasure and financial loss to the Marling squires" (*MH* 5) sets the scene in *Marling Hall*.   Charles Belton asks covetously, "Why haven't I a rich aunt with fixed basins?" (*TH* 23). As *The Headmistress* revolves around the Beltons', and others', change in status, an apposite line shows "Miss Pettinger . . . joining in the chorus with the air of Coriolanus trying to be friendly with the plebeians" (*TH* 230). Over his small charges' boxing prowess, "Mason (Southbridge School's boxing instructor) wore a transfigured expression which may possibly have been approached by St. John on Patmos" (*HR* 154). Most of the incongruities concern manners, this one about the contents of the Brandons' aunt's will: "The rest of the company, while thinking poorly of such open curiosity, were greatly relieved that anyone had little enough fine feeling to ask what by this time they were all burning to know" (*TB* 192).

Like E. M. Delafield and her predilection for metonymy and for distinguishing a character throughout with an appropriate name: "pink *beret* drank tea" (*PLL*) and two aptly named male characters, "Casabianca," the steadfast tutor (*PLL*) and "Agrippa," the desk-confined civil service man (*PLW*), Thirkell capitalizes on metonymy. Her everyday "Laverings and the White House all sat in chairs on the terrace and drank what they fancied" (*BL* 170) is outshone by Alice Barton's irresistible "Collins" to Lady Pomfret. In *Pomfret Towers* the butcher is "Mr. Bones," as Sally's dogs and other dogs figure largely in the novel, and appropriate woolly names are attached to the Barsetshire villages: Skeynes, Winter Overcotes, Winter Underclose. In *August Folly* even the local pubs are the Woolpack and The Ram and Twins.

Thirkell's humor is never limited; serendipitous plays on words, phrases, and institutions abound. "(Postmistress) Miss Phipps's inquisitions into the mail bag" (*BL* 17) is one. In fitting nautical terms, Admiral Palliser, now retired, deals with a waste pipe blockage: "having grappled his prize, sheared off, hauling as he went . . . " (*MB* 87); daughter, Jane Gresham, does not like him to "quarterdeck" the servants; and "Captain Hornby at once tacked to the opposite side of the street, cruised along in front of the newsagent . . . put his helm hard over and had Elsa safely back on their own side of the road again before Mrs. Hunter could turn her prow for a stern chase. This masterly piece of maneuvering brought them up under the lee of

Dowlah Cottage . . . " (*TH* 189). Although Jane Austen is more mocking in describing Anne Elliot's thoughts about Captain Wentworth as she walks in Bath, "Prettier musings of high-wrought love and eternal constancy, could never have passed along the streets of Bath, than Anne was sporting with . . . . It was almost enough to spread purification and perfume all the way" (*P* 192), she does not use such language to steal the scene from Anne and Captain Wentworth in their reuniting walk up the town. Thirkell too reserves the nautical terms for a congenial, everyday walk by the newly engaged couple, not for their reconciliation.

Some characters have *motifs*. Whenever Richard Tebben appears or is discussed, his ears are mentioned: when it comes to a leading role in *Hippolytus*, the village pageant that summer, ". . . in (Mrs. Palmer's) opinion, anyone whose ears stuck out as much as Richard's was naturally disqualified for a part which did not demand a wig" (*AF* 15), and at the Woolpack at closing time, "'Young Richard would make a good turn with that old Neddy of theirs,' said Bert to his audience. 'I'd laugh like anything to see them both wagging their ears'" (46). Apropos of Richard's being attracted to Mrs. Dean's presence as a moth to a flame, "Rachel looked up and saw, romantically surrounded by wistaria and honeysuckle, its large ears clearly outlined against the moonlight, the silhouette of Richard's head" (44); and "His flushed, earnest face and urgent ears pleaded so strongly for him that Mrs. Dean relented . . . " (88).

Like Benson and Delafield, Thirkell is a reader, and her authorial language reflects her wide reading, education, and culture. A construction peculiar to her is brilliant Laminate parody. Her earliest and perhaps her finest set piece depicts the meeting between Daphne Stonor, who cares for young Mr. Bond, and Betty Dean, who once played Phaedra to his Hippolytus:

> As when two bulls of milk-white fleece, ranging the slopes of Aileron Timavus, espy afar off the heifer, grazing, ah! beneath the ilex whose cold shadow the careful farmer will avoid to seek as roof for the golden swarm lest haply the

stored sweetness of the honey turn to maleficent vinegar baneful as the Centaur's blood on the fatal shirt doomed to lead the club-bearer to the gloomy realms of Dis, anon they paw the ground with equal foot, this flashing forth fire from his eyes as the careful husbandman strikes the spark from tinder . . . .(*BL* 226)

Another *tour de force* is George Knox's analysis of Awfully Dull Novels:

> They appear to me to be divided into two classes—obscene, and . . . historical . . . my hero shall be an ardent student of philosophy, a follower of Spinoza, Kant, Plato . . . modern craze for education . . . the lot (done) so philosophically that hundreds and thousands of readers will feel that they are improving their minds by reading philosophy, which is just as harsh and crabbed as the dull fools suppose, until it is made attractive by the lure of sex. (*HR* 270)

In her review of *High Rising* at the time, Louise Field comments, "It cannot truthfully be said that George Knox's discourses on modern fiction . . . have any bearing on the plot, the characters, or anything else in the novel, but who could fail to chuckle over (them)."[21]

Virginia Woolf's analysis of Jane Austen's social satire in her creation of characters, "She encircles them with the lash of a whip-like phrase which, as it runs round them, cuts out their silhouettes for ever. But there they remain; no excuse is made for them and no mercy shown them,"[22] applies equally to Thirkell. One of Thirkell's best achievements of caricature through language is Mrs. Major Spender and her monologues:

> I simply didn't know what to do, I mean Ockley's Hotel where I always go and all the staff are devoted to me and the manager almost a personal friend if you know what I mean who has known us all for years was blown up practically under my eyes . . . . So I said, Not for you, my girl, and went to my club and sent a wire to Bobbie over the 'phone. How the telegram got delivered I cannot tell, said she in a resigned voice, for one knows what telegrams are now . . . . (*NR* 77)

Mrs. Spender makes her reaction to a wartime bombing sound insincere. Her confiding in complete strangers as to her husband's woolliness, with asides, stage directions, and *I means*, inanely focuses the attention on herself rather than on the surrounding devastation. Thirkell frames one of those monologues with a brilliantly scathing Celtic triad uttered by a soldier-scholar associate of Major Spender:

> 'The three Evil Colours of Britain,' Captain Powell-Jones announced, looking fixedly at Mrs. Spender.
> 'The colour of the peacock on a woman's head-gear,
> The colour of the salmon on a woman's mouth,
> The colour of the Saxon's blood on a woman's fingers.' (276)

A shorter set piece of heightened language picks up one of Thirkell's threads in the novels: parallel family lines. Her Margetts, Pattens, and Polletts, who take pride in running the trains, are at least as old as the landed aristocracy of the Bonds and the Palmers: "No trains can proceed until their various drivers have exchanged uncouth tokens of metal, like pot-hooks and hangers, or gigantic nose and ear-rings to be bartered with savage tribes for diamonds and gold . . . ." (*AF* 5). And on the land, the credit for the new calf of the prize-winning Lily Langtry goes not to Mr. Middleton, gentleman farmer, but to his man, Pucken, who earlier "shouted some pre-Conquest instructions to his horse" (*BL* 5).

Thirkell also uses her authorial voice to make a sly comment about the dinners of Mr. Oriel, the Vicar, that contains an oblique allusion to an earlier masculine tradition, and also mocks those critics who have claimed that Jane Austen never shows a scene devoid of women:

> As a rule he gave his men a very short interval in which to discuss whatever it is that men discuss when left together; high politics and dashing days in the hunting field, or the Odes of Horace, we would like to think, though finding ourselves unable to do so with conviction. (*TH* 82)

Her novels abound with literary references, including informed discussions of John Donne, Bohun, and le Capet, that become vehicles for mocking the pretensions of the male writers—Hilary Grant, Geoffrey Harvey, Oliver Marling—and their techniques for securing an admiring female audience. Thirkell also salutes Jane Austen, with amusing references that knowledgeable readers would recognize. After the houseparty at Pomfret Towers, Alice Barton "wrote a handsome Collins to Lady Pomfret in which she expressed the hope that everyone was well" (216). In *August Folly*, "Susan and Robin (Dean) . . . took a second to the hymns in the manner of Mr. Frank Churchill, slightly, but correctly" (196), a reference to Jane Austen's *Emma* that is repeated in "Captain Barclay even providing like Mr. Frank Churchill a slight but correct second" (*MH* 185).

Another allusion to Jane Austen tells both hero and heroine something endearing about each other:

> 'Your respected mamma,' said Laurence to Margaret . . . 'is telling my Aunt Palmer exactly where she gets off at about the veils for the chorus.' 'Yes, mother is a little like Mrs. Norris sometimes.' As Laurence didn't answer, she wondered if he had perhaps never heard of Miss Austen, blamed herself for the ungenerous thought, then just to make herself plain, added nervously, 'Miss Austen, I mean.' 'Well, it does my heart good to hear you say Miss Austen like that,' said Laurence . . . . 'People who say Jane or talk about Janeites revolt me. The sort that can walk with kings and not lose that common touch. "Miss Austen to you" is what I feel inclined to say. . . .' (*AF* 165, 66)

No other allusions to Jane Austen appear until *Miss Bunting* (1946), the title character's last stint as governess: Miss Bunting's "reading aloud to (Anne Fielding) in the evenings from the works of . . . Miss Austen" had "lighted a candle" for sixteen-year-old Anne (38). Her characters' holding onto classic English literature and what were traditional topics of discussion for the educated gentry may be Thirkell's attempt to maintain social standards at the end of the war in the face of such forces as the Mr. Adamses.

With language, Thirkell creates characters who throughout the years of these novels—1934 to 1945—portray her three or four families as the backbone of England; servicemen recognized this and wrote to tell her so. The Marling family members are reassuringly typecast by their speech and their interests. Mrs. Marling's questions at breakfast time show her to be an autocrat, an organizer, whether others like it or not. Mr. Marling is as busy with county work as she, and he knows the land—the correct disposal of Pook's Piece—which is vital for England. Daughter Lucy Marling's ready "I'll tell you what" shows her own willingness to shoulder responsibility. Like Lydia Keith, Lucy takes over the farm while her brothers, Robert and Oliver, are in the Army or engaged in other vital work. Lucy's older sister, Lettice Watson, is a young widow, a mother, and a Red Cross worker. She is less than high-powered, but she is well-bred, and the reader is reassured to hear that "a Browning title, 'A Bean Stripe; also Apple Eating,' floated into her mind" (*MH* 24). Miss Bunting and the children's nurses are also shown as the backbone of England, civilizing its young, and the entire household is seen to be fighting red tape engendered by know-nothings. Since it is wartime, the village of Marling absorbs two strangers, Frances and Geoffrey Harvey, who are seconded to the Barsetshire Regional Commissioner's Office from London, and who are far from backbone. When "Miss Harvey said with the easy condescension of a university woman that David's thesis was reducible to a very simple arithmetical formula . . . " (284), the reader is confident that Frances Harvey will not "land" Oliver Marling and stay in the provinces, because she has now been linked by language with the disliked Miss Pettinger, whose behavior at a prewar summer tea party is slyly disparaged: "(She) broke in upon a quiet talk that Everard was having with Mr. Birkett . . . and drew them into the conversation with the easy tact of a university woman" (*SH* 310).

Charles put the "two shillings supplied by Mr. Belton (into) . . . the embroidered Liberty-green lozenge-shaped bag supported on a kind of small ecclesiastical turned broom handle." (TH 31)

Thirkell's novels are not set in an ascertainable region, as the Austen novels are. While fictional Highbury's location has been traced on a map, Thirkell's Barsetshire is not real: she has borrowed it wholesale from

Anthony Trollope. Nonetheless, her characters are real, and her approach to social satire lies in the buildup of the surroundings, or, alternatively, lack of such detail. In contrast, Jane Austen creates an artful *illusion* of place and of things, but in reality most spatial details have been pruned and polished away for the sake of the author's art. In the Northanger Abbey guest room Catherine Morland projects a determinedly Gothic view onto some articles of furniture, and the reader sees Fanny Price's unheated East room at Mansfield Park through the cataloguing of her geraniums, her books, her writing-desk, a faded footstool that is the former artistic work of Julia Bertram, and numerous work-boxes given to Fanny by her cousin Tom, all now treasured because of their associations. At Hartfield, Emma has been able to replace "the small-sized Pembroke" with a "large modern circular table" (*E* 347). But these particulars are exceptions to Jane Austen's economical descriptions.

In the Thirkell novels there is a strong sense of place, typically achieved by detailed description. Seen through Denis Stonor's eyes, the pre-war Skeynes railroad station is a period piece:

> the stationmaster had a little office chokingly heated by a stove with a red-hot iron chimney and furnished with yellowing crackling documents impaled on spikes; . . . the porters had a room called Lamps which was always locked; and at the end of the down platform was a tank on four legs from which local engines still obtained their water supply through a leathern hose pipe . . . . Denis . . . strolled up to a chocolate machine and actually obtained a small slab of very nasty pink chocolate cream . . . . (*BL* 27)

His sister, Daphne, looks forward to a view of Lady Bond's church-going hat: "A massive erection of brown velvet crowned with the produce of field, flood, and grove, it was perched high on its wearer's head with fine disregard of fashion" (*BL* 77). Such frequent bucolic gatherings as Thirkell's squires, the backbone of England, standing around the pig pens scratching their pigs' backs and talking with their cowmen about others' prize cows, are not to be found in the Austen novels—although that may have been how

Mr. Knightley learned of Robert Martin's feelings for Harriet Smith. Lou Pucken, daughter of Sarah Pucken who had been a kitchenmaid at Staple Park, is baptized Lucasta after Lady Bond (*BL*); Palmyra Phipps, who as keeper of the post office and telephone exchange is linked to everyone, is named after Mrs. Palmer of the Manor House. The post office and the telephone exchange are gathering places and centers of information, the women who staff them constituting part of the ring of services that provides a buffer for the gentry. *Before Lunch* is framed by this service, beginning with a precise description that makes it human and guileless:

> Mrs. Middleton had long ago accepted Miss Phipps's inquisitions into the mail bag and was indeed inclined to admire her unerring memory for every correspondent's handwriting. Miss Phipps took the broadest view of His Majesty's Post Office regulations and would always keep letters back at the shop instead of sending them up to Laverings if Mr. Middleton telephoned that he was going up to town by the early train and would call in for his. More than once had she allowed him to hunt through the bag for his own letters, open them and alter a word or figure . . . . As she had never put her power and knowledge to any but kindly uses no complaint had ever been made and the Inspector, though he vaguely suspected something, could not put his finger on it. (14)

The novel ends with Daphne Stonor successfully prevailing upon Miss Phipps to let her have Lady Bond's letters back from the mailbag, and then Mrs. Middleton making a similar last moment request.

Miss Phipps's knowledge extends beyond the Post Office door: "if Laverings wanted to ring up any neighbour she always knew if the person wanted was at home, calling on a neighbour, or shopping at Winter Overcotes where the chemist could take a message" (14). Similarly, in *The Headmistress* written six years later, when Heather Adams falls through thin ice on the lake and Mrs. Belton tries to "ring" Miss Sparling at Harefield School at the same time that Miss Sparling is trying to reach her, the operator, Gertie Pilson, "who already knew more about the accident than either of these ladies," tells Miss Sparling to put down her receiver and she will put the call through (*TH* 272).

"Perhaps in 1950 when Lady Agnes Graham presents the girls at court
. . . Marling Hall will be not only hilarious reading but required reading
for all social historians."[23]

In her comedy of manners novels, Thirkell has created and recorded and
gently satirized a world that was familiar to her contemporary readers,
bringing to life a world not only unfamiliar, but otherwise lost to the modern
reader. In 1941 *High Rising* is already described as "an engaging picture of
a kind of life that has now suffered total eclipse"[24]; and in 1956 *Time and
Tide* recognizes the significance of her capturing of time and place: "the
Barsetshire stories . . . set out a pattern of a certain sort of English life in the
first half of the twentieth century, which social historians of the future would
be foolish not to follow."[25]

Conclusion

From Mr. Collins to Lucia, The Provincial Lady, Robert, and Old Mrs. Blenkinsop, and Mrs. Major Spender, the standard of characterization set by these comedy of manners writers has remained supremely high. Through inspired language they have established and maintained a polished tradition of social satire. Their shades of humor range from the irony of Jane Austen's exquisite classic prose, its origins in the eighteenth century, to Mrs. Gaskell's gentler humor and the unexpected incongruities of the Provincial Lady Diaries, Benson's exaggerations and fresh applications of word play, and Thirkell's wit and dash of malice in revealing a character's social class and degree of education and culture through language and speech patterns.

The comedy of manners novels of Benson, Delafield, and Thirkell capture the fashions and foibles that had endured for the more than 100 years since Jane Austen. Scenes and characters echo and mirror each other across time and space, attesting to the enduring nature of the conventions that ordered the behavior of those who once were the bulwark of English society. Such conventions concerning food, clothing, and attitudes, with the social roles of observing and enforcing them almost automatically assumed by such village principals as the clergymen, the landed gentry, their sons and heirs and their wives and daughters, as well as the servants, are properly seen as comedy by their audience of contemporary readers. People perennially recognize each other and themselves in the pervasively and beguilingly witty situations.

These novels also convey a picture of women's place in society, offering a satirical view of a world not usually of the reader's making. Such a view has not been encouraged for many years. Feminists have been too serious and have had too much at stake to rely on or encourage humor as a sword or shield. In this study we note that humor is, and has been, a woman's way of rising above an unsatisfactory marriage, lack of money, and other situations that are less gratifying than she would have liked. Referring to *Cranford*, Spacks says that the humor stems from "women surmount(ing) the restrictions of their lot by making the minute momentous. So little is at stake in all their concerns."[1] While both Delafield and Thirkell have established themselves as writers with a comic view of life, Delafield is a feminist despite the Provincial Lady's frequent asides on not letting Robert hear, while Thirkell presents a conservative view of women almost exclusively defined by the family.

What is the future of the comedy of manners? Upon their reissue in the 1970s and 1980s, the novels of these three modern heirs of Jane Austen won the admiration and appreciation of a new generation of readers, who might well concur with Orville Prescott's 1945 sociological as well as literary comment on Thirkell's *The Headmistress:* "The gentle and smiling humor is thoroughly engaging. It depends on a highly civilized point of view, and has not the faintest resemblance to the all too prevalent humor of wisecracks, vulgarity, farce and near insanity."[2] These readers might also agree with Thirkell herself in liking novels that made her laugh,[3] for while irony has been regarded as more characteristic of English writers, its subtle humor not easily translated into the American idiom, American readers nevertheless recognize both themselves and others in the characters. And even though the comedy of manners novels are not best known for *plot*, a third element in their revival is the universal longing for a well-told story, resulting in renewed interest in the novel as a literary form. Most important, these novels reflect balance and order in a society whose values are exemplified by the concept that good manners count more than money. According to Spacks, and borne out by example, "Manners cope with exigencies of money and class."[4]

While these comedy of manners novels in the Jane Austen tradition may have been in eclipse since the 1940s, their resurgence speaks for itself. Time, after all, may be the best literary critic.

Notes

Introduction

1   Norman Page, "The Great Tradition Revisited," in *Jane Austen's Achievement*, ed. Juliet McMaster (New York: Harper, 1976) 44–63. Forster said that "from Jane Austen he learned 'the possibilities of domestic humour'" 59.

2   M. Abrams, *A Glossary of Literary Terms* (New York: Holt, 1981) 26.

3   Harold Bloom, Introduction, *Jane Austen: Modern Critical Views*, ed. Harold Bloom (New York: Chelsea, 1986) 1.

4   Bloom 2.

5   Jan Fergus, *Jane Austen and the Didactic Novel* (Totowa: Barnes, 1983) 8.

6   Fergus 9.

7   R. W. Chapman, *Jane Austen: Facts and Problems* (London: Oxford UP, 1970), 152.

8   *Glossary of Literary Terms* 168.

9   B. C. Southam, *Jane Austen: The Critical Heritage*, vol. 2 (New York: Routledge, 1987) 108.

10 Virginia Woolf, "Jane Austen," *The Common Reader* (New York: Harcourt: Harvest, 1953) 143, 4.

11 Edgar Wright, *Mrs. Gaskell: The Basis for Reassessment* (London: Oxford, 1965) 104.

12 Wright 20.

13 J. B. Priestley, *The English Comic Character* (London: Bodley, 1925) 158.

14 Priestley 167.

15 Priestley, *English Humour* (New York: Stein, 1976) 115.

16 J. B. Priestley, *The English Comic Character* (London: Bodley, 1925) 160.

17 O'Brien x–xi.

18 Maurice McCullen, *E. M. Delafield* (Boston: Twayne, 1985) 53.

E. F. Benson

1 Nancy Mitford, Introduction, *Make Way for Lucia*, by E. F. Benson (New York: Harper, 1977) 7.

2 B. C. Southam, *Jane Austen: The Critical Heritage*, vol. 2 (New York: Routledge, 1987) 64.

3 R. W. Chapman, *Jane Austen: Facts and Problems* (London: Oxford UP, 1970) 134.

4 Stephen Pile, Introduction. *Mrs. Ames*, by E. F. Benson (London: Hogarth, 1985) ii.

5 Mitford 5.

6 Gilbert Seldes, Introduction. *All About Lucia*, by E. F. Benson (Garden City: Doubleday, 1936) x.

7 J.B. Priestley, *The English Comic Character* (London: Bodley, 1925) 158.

8 Louis Kronenberger, rev. of *The Diary of a Provincial Lady*, by E. M. Delafield. *New York Times*. IV 18 Oct. 1931: 4:2.

9 Beatrice Sherman, rev. of *Marling Hall*, by Angela Thirkell, *New York Times* VI 4 Oct. 1942: 14:5.

10 Rebecca West, who was on the board of the English weekly literary journal *Time and Tide* in the 1920s and 1930s, commented, "The vogue of . . . *The Dolly Dialogues* transcends anything our generation has known in the extent to which these books dominated the public mind of their time." *Ending in Earnest: A Literary Log* (Garden City: Doubleday, 1931) 87.

11 Rev. of *The Dolly Dialogues*, by Anthony Hope, *New York Times* 11 Nov. 1894: 23.

12 Pile ii.

13 E. M. Delafield, "The Diary of a Provincial Lady," in *Titles to Fame*, ed. Denys Killian Roberts (London: Nelson, 1937) 131.

14 R. Ellis Roberts, Obituary, E. F. Benson, *New York Times* 19 Oct. 1940: 19–20.

15 Rev. of *Mapp and Lucia*, by E. F. Benson. (Originally in) *Literary Digest* 18 Sept. 1920: 101, *Twentieth Century Literary Criticism* 27, ed. Dennis Poupard (Detroit: Gale, 1988) 1.

16 Cynthia and Tony Reavell, *E. F. Benson, Mr. Benson remembered in Rye, and the world of Tilling* (London: Headley, Invicta, 1984) 69.

17 Reavell 69.

18 Pile iv.

19 V. S. Pritchett, "E. F. Benson: Fairy Tales," in *The Tale Bearers* (New York: Random, 1980) 18.

20 Mitford 8.

21   Auberon Waugh, rev. of *Make Way for Lucia*, by E. F. Benson. *New York Times* VI 7 Aug. 1977:1.

22   Mitford 8.

23   Reavell 67.

24   Patricia Meyer Spacks, *Gossip* (New York: Knopf, 1985) 165–70.

25   Micheal Mac Liammoir, Foreword, *Lucia's Progress (The Worshipful Lucia)*, by E. F. Benson (London: Heinemann, 1967) ix.

26   Richard Jones, "Life Imitating Art?" *Christian Science Monitor* 21 Oct. 1986: 39.

27   Reavell 67.

28   John Updike, "Books," *The New Yorker* 30 Aug. 1990: 86.

29   Critic Edgar Wright comments that a "minor theme in all Mrs. Gaskell's work is the power of a woman to get things done, if necessary at the expense of a man," as "Jem Hearn, the joiner whose bachelor days are unceremoniously cut short so that he can set up house to provide a home for Martha's mistress, acquiesces with hardly a demur." Edgar Wright, *Mrs. Gaskell* (Great Britain: Oxford UP, 1965) 112; 112n.

30   W. H. Auden, "Letter to Lord Byron," qtd. in *Collected Poems*, ed. Edward Mendelson (New York: Random, 1976).

E. M. Delafield

1   Elaine Showalter, *A Literature of Their Own: British Women Novelists from Brontë to Lessing* (Princeton: Princeton UP, 1977) 8.

2   Showalter 13.

3   Showalter 299, 300.

4   E. M. Delafield, "The Diary of a Provincial Lady," in *Titles to Fame*, ed. Denys Killian Roberts (London: Nelson, 1937) 123.

5   Delafield, "The Diary of a Provincial Lady," 125–6.

6   Patricia Meyer Spacks, qtd. in Showalter 8.

7   Lloyd W. Brown, "The Business of Marrying and Mothering," in *Jane Austen's Achievement*, ed. Juliet McMaster (London: Hamilton, 1976) 33.

8   Louis Kronenberger, rev. of *The Diary of a Provincial Lady*, by E. M. Delafield, *New York Times*. IV 18 Oct. 1931: 4:2.

9   Margaret Lawrence, "Sophisticated Ladies," in *School of Femininity* (Port Washington: Kennikat, 1936) 302.

10   Delafield, "The Diary of a Provincial Lady," 126.

11   Maurice McCullen, *E. M. Delafield* (Boston: Twayne, 1985) 18. In 1937 Harold Macmillan, Delafield's publisher, was reported as saying that "E. M. Delafield had gone to America again—that she wrote too many books for financial reasons & they were helping her to make the

intervals longer." (Vera Brittain, *Chronicle of Friendship: Diary of the Thirties: 1932–1939*, ed. Alan Bishop (London: Gollancz, 1986) 304.

12   Delafield, "The Diary of a Provincial Lady," 128.

13   Vicountess Margaret Rhondda (Margaret Thomas), "E. M. Delafield," *Time and Tide* 13 Dec. 1947: 1346.

14   Kate O'Brien, Foreword. *The Provincial Lady*, by E. M. Delafield (London: Macmillan, 1947) x–xi.

15   McCullen 60.

16   Kronenberger IV 4:2.

17   Lawrence 302.

18   Lawrence 302–3.

19   Mary Evans, *Jane Austen and the State* (New York: Routledge, 1987) 62–3.

20   Evans 38.

21   Lawrence 302.

22   Brittain 91.

23   Brittain 103.

24   McCullen 60.

25   Kronenberger IV 4: 2.

26   Kronenberger IV 4: 2.

27   Henry Seidel Canby, rev. of *The Diary of a Provincial Lady*, by E. M. Delafield, *Saturday Review of Literature* 14 Jan. 1933: 376.

28   Canby 376.

29   Jane Spence Southron, rev. of *The Provincial Lady in Wartime*, by E. M. Delafield, *New York Times* VI 7 Apr. 1940: 9.

30   Eric Gillett, "The English Literary Scene, 1954," *Essays by Divers Hands: Being the Transactions of the Royal Society of Literature* XXX, ed. N. Hardy Wallis (London: Oxford UP, 1960) 132.

31   David Daiches, *The Present Age in British Literature* (Bloomington: Indiana UP, 1958) 281–2.

32   A question on the BBC quiz program "My Word": "What do Pepys, the Provincial Lady, and *The Diary of a Nobody* have in common?" Antonia Fraser replied, "Every day in every way they wrote everything in their diaries." South Africa, June 27, 1990.

33   Miss Read (Dora Jessie Saint), *Village Diary* (London: Joseph, 1957) 232.

34   Miss Read, *No Holly for Miss Quinn* (London: Joseph, 1976) 94.

35   Delafield 131.

36   E. M. Delafield, Introduction, *The British Character: Studied and Revealed by Pont* (Graham Laidler) (London: Collins, 1938) 9.

37   Delafield, Pont 9.

38   Delafield, Pont 6.

39 Delafield, Pont 9. The Reverend Mr. George Austen, Jane Austen's father, was Oxonian.

40 Kronenberger IV 4: 2.

41 Delafield, "Diary of a Provincial Lady" 127.

42 Delafield, "Diary of a Provincial Lady" 138.

43 McCullen 59.

44 Winifred Holtby, *Letters to a Friend*, ed. Alice Holtby and Jean McWilliam (London: Collins, 1937) 435.

45 Brittain 203.

46 Carolyn G. Heilbron, *Writing a Woman's Life* (New York: Norton, 1988) 105.

47 Lady Rhondda 1346.

48 Margaret McDowell, "'E. M. Delafield,' British Novelists, 1890–1928: Traditionalists," *Dictionary of Literary Biography* 34, ed. Thomas F. Staley (Detroit: Bruccoli, 1985) 94.

49 McCullen 91.

50 Brittain 51.

51 Margaret Drabble, "Three Cheers for a Woman of Sensibility," *The Jane Austen Society Report for 1989* 9.

Angela Thirkell

1 Louise Maunsell Field, rev. of *Pomfret Towers*, by Angela Thirkell, *New York Times*. VI 23 Oct.1938: 7:2.

2 Field, rev. of *The Brandons*, by Angela Thirkell, *New York Times*. V 25 June 1939: 1.

3 Field, rev. of *Before Lunch*, by Angela Thirkell, *New York Times*. VI 2 June 1940: 5:2.

4 Field, rev. of *Northbridge Rectory*, by Angela Thirkell, *New York Times*. VI 1942: 7.

5 Orville Prescott, rev. of *The Headmistress*, by Angela Thirkell, *New York Times*. VI 22 Jan. 1945: 15:2.

6 Graham McInnes, *The Road to Gundegai* (London: Hogarth, 1985).

7 Robertson Davies, Introduction, *The Road to Gundegai*, by Graham McInnes (London: Hogarth, 1985).

8 Field, "High Rising," VI 7:2.

9 Field, "High Rising," VI 7:3.

10 Field, "Before Lunch," VI 5:2.

11 Prescott VI 15:2.

12 Isabelle Mallet, rev. of *Growing Up*, by Angela Thirkell, *New York Times*. VII 13 Feb. 1944: 3:1.

13   Margaret Drabble, "Three Cheers for a Woman of Sensibility," in *The Jane Austen Society Report for 1989.* 9.

14   Maggie Lane, *Jane Austen and Food* (London: Hambledon, 1995) 146.

15   Adrian Coates, in Thirkell's *High Rising* (1933), "is Hamish Hamilton (1900–), founder in 1931 and managing director until 1972 of the London publishing house which bears his name." William Amos, *The Originals: Who's Really Who in Fiction* (London: Cape, 1985) 111.

16   Margot Strickland, *Angela Thirkell: Portrait of a Lady Novelist.* (London: Duckworth, 1977) 78.

17   Field, "Pomfret Towers," VI 7:2.

18   Patricia Meyer Spacks, *Gossip* (New York: Knopf, 1985) 189.

19   Spacks 189.

20   Thirkell was very pleased with herself for inventing "ackcherly," which was said to delight fans when she lectured, and she told P. P. Howe, Hamish Hamilton's partner, that *The Headmistress* "is so like the rest, except for Heather Adams of whom I ackcherly found myself getting quite fond." Margot Strickland, *Angela Thirkell: Portrait of a Lady Novelist* (London: Duckworth, 1977) 138.

21   Field, "High Rising," VI 7:3.

22   Virginia Woolf, *The Common Reader* (New York: Harcourt: Harvest) 143, 144.

23   Leo Lerman, Rev. of *High Rising*, by Angela Thirkell, *Saturday Review of Literature* 31 Oct. 1942: 25:15.

24   Field, "High Rising," VI 7:3.

25   C. A. Lejeune, "Angela Thirkell," *Time and Tide* 9 June 1956: 685.

Epilogue

Thank you for reading this perspective celebrating Jane Austen and her modern heirs.

Having experienced the triumph—"Drop that and read this!"—of discovering another author in a favorite style, I prompt you to delve further into the works of these delightful writers.

Bibliography

Primary Sources

Austen, Jane. *Emma*. 1816. Ed. R. W. Chapman. Oxford UP, 1965.

——. *Letters*. Ed. R. W. Chapman. London: Oxford UP, 1952. No. 76, 77, 80, 100, 133, 134.

——. *Mansfield Park*. 1814. Ed. R. W. Chapman. London: Oxford UP, 1965.

——. *Northanger Abbey*. 1818. Ed. R. W. Chapman. London: Oxford UP, 1965.

——. *Persuasion*. 1818. Ed. R. W. Chapman. London: Oxford UP, 1965.

——. *Pride and Prejudice*. 1813. Ed. R. W. Chapman. London: Oxford UP, 1965.

——. *Sense and Sensibility*. 1811. Ed. R. W. Chapman. London: Oxford UP, 1965.

Benson, E. F. *Final Edition: Informal Autobiography*. London: Longmans, 1940.

——. *Lucia in London*. 1927. New York: Harper, 1977.

——. *Mapp and Lucia*. 1931. New York: Harper, 1977.

——. *Miss Mapp*. 1923. New York: Harper, 1977.

——. *Queen Lucia*. 1920. New York: Harper, 1977.

——. *Trouble for Lucia*. 1939. New York: Harper, 1977.

——. *The Worshipful Lucia*. 1936. New York: Harper, 1977.

Delafield, E. M. (Edmée Elizabeth Monica de la Pasture Dashwood). *The Diary of a Provincial Lady*. 1930. London: Baker, 1969.

——. "The Diary of a Provincial Lady." *Titles to Fame*. Ed. Denys Killian Roberts. London: Nelson, 1937. 121–138.

——. Introduction. *The British Character: Studied and Revealed by Pont* (Graham Laidler). London: Collins, 1938. 7–10.

——. *The Provincial Lady in America*. 1934. Acad. Chicago, 1983.

——. *The Provincial Lady in London*. 1932. Acad. Chicago, 1982.

——. *The Provincial Lady in Wartime*. 1940. Acad. Chicago, 1984.

Gaskell, Elizabeth. *Cranford*. 1853. Ed. Elizabeth Porges Watson. Oxford: Oxford UP, 1980.

Hope, Anthony. (Sir Anthony Hope Hawkins). *The Dolly Dialogues*. 1891. London: Methuen, 1926.

Thirkell, Angela. *August Folly*. 1936. New York: Carroll, 1988.

——. *Before Lunch*. New York: Knopf, 1940.

——. *The Brandons*. New York: Knopf, 1939.

——. *Cheerfulness Breaks In*. New York: Knopf, 1941.

——. *Growing Up*. New York: Knopf, 1944.

——. *The Headmistress*. New York: Knopf, 1945.

——. *High Rising*. New York: Knopf, 1935.

——. *Marling Hall*. New York: Knopf, 1942.

——. *Miss Bunting*. New York: Knopf, 1946. New York: Pyramid, 1972.

——. *Northbridge Rectory*. New York: Knopf, 1942.

——. *Pomfret Towers*. New York: Knopf, 1938.

———. *Summer Half.* New York: Knopf, 1937.

———. *Wild Strawberries.* New York: Knopf, 1934.

Secondary Sources

Abrams, M. H. *A Glossary of Literary Terms.* New York: Holt, 1981.

Amos, William. *The Originals: Who's Really Who in Fiction.* London: Cape, 1985. (Also published as *The Originals: A-Z of Fiction's Real-life Characters.* Boston: Little, 1985)

Auden, W. H. "Letter to Lord Byron." *Collected Poems.* Ed. Edward Mendelson. New York: Random, 1976

Bliven, Naomi. "Portrait of the Young Man as an Artist." *The New Yorker* 26 Mar. 1990: 94.

Bloom, Harold. Introduction. *Jane Austen: Modern Critical Views.* Ed. Harold Bloom. New York: Chelsea, 1986.

Brittain, Vera. *Chronicle of Friendship: Diary of the Thirties: 1932-1939.* Ed. Alan Bishop. London: Gollancz, 1986.

Brown, Lloyd W. "The Business of Marrying and Mothering." *Jane Austen's Achievement.* Ed. Juliet McMaster. London: Macmillan, 1976. 27–43.

Calder, Angus. *The People's War: Britain 1939–1945.* New York: Pantheon, 1969.

Canby, Henry Seidel. Rev. of *The Diary of a Provincial Lady*, by E. M. Delafield. *Saturday Review of Literature* 14 Jan. 1933: 376.

Cunningham, Valentine. *British Writers of the Thirties.* Oxford: Oxford UP, 1988.

Daiches, David. *The Present Age in British Literature.* Bloomington: Indiana UP, 1958.

Davies, Robertson. Introduction. *The Road to Gundegai*, by Graham McInnes. London: Hogarth, 1985.

De Kay, Drake. Rev. of *Summer Half,* by Angela Thirkell. *New York Times* VI 5 June 1938: 6: 4.

Delafield, E. M., Herbert Morrison, and Howard Spring. *This War We Wage.* New York: Emerson, 1941.

Rev. of *The Diary of a Provincial Lady,* by E. M. Delafield. *Boston Transcript* 3 Oct. 1931: 1.

Rev. of *The Diary of a Provincial Lady,* by E. M. Delafield. *New York Times Book Review* 8 Aug. 1982: 24.

Rev. of *The Dolly Dialogues,* by Anthony Hope. *New York Times* 11 Nov. 1894: 23.

Drabble, Margaret. "Three Cheers for a Woman of Sensibility." *The Jane Austen Society Report for 1989.* 9.

Evans, Mary. *Jane Austen and the State.* New York: Routledge, 1987.

Fergus, Jan. *Jane Austen and the Didactic Novel.* Totowa: Barnes & Noble, 1983.

Field, Louise Maunsell. Rev. of *Before Lunch,* by Angela Thirkell. *New York Times* VI 2 June 1940: 5:2.

——. Rev. of *The Brandons,* by Angela Thirkell. *New York Times* VI 25 June 1939:1.

——. Rev. of *High Rising,* by Angela Thirkell. *New York Times* VI 28 Sept. 1941: 7:3.

——. Rev. of *Northbridge Rectory,* by Angela Thirkell. *New York Times* VI 11 Jan. 1942: 6–7.

——. Rev. of *Pomfret Towers,* by Angela Thirkell. *New York Times* VI 23 Oct. 1938: 7:2.

Gillett, Eric. "The English Literary Scene, 1954." *Essays by Divers Hands: Being the Transactions of the Royal Society of Literature* XXX. Ed. N. Hardy Wallis. London: Oxford UP, 1960. 130–133.

———. "E. M. Delafield." *The London Mercury* Dec. 1932: 170. Rpt. in Ruth Z. Temple and Martin Tucker, ed. *A Library of Literary Criticism. Modern British Literature I.* New York: Ungar, 1966. 131.

Green, Martin. "1945–1951: Exile and the Decay of Hope." *Children of the Sun: A Narrative of "Decadence" in England After 1918.* New York: Basic Books, 1976. 347–381.

Heilbron, Carolyn G. *Writing a Woman's Life.* New York: Norton, 1988. 104–5.

Holtby, Winifred. *Letters to a Friend.* Ed. Alice Holtby and Jean McWilliam. London: Collins, 1937. 435.

Jones, Richard. "Life Imitating Art?" *The Christian Science Monitor* 21 Oct. 1986: 39.

Kennedy, Margaret. *Where Stands a Winged Sentry.* New Haven: Yale UP, 1941.

Kronenberger, Louis. Rev. of *The Diary of a Provincial Lady*, by E. M. Delafield. *New York Times* IV 18 Oct. 1931: 4: 2.

———. Rev. of *The Provincial Lady in London*, by E. M. Delafield. *New York Times* V 22 Jan. 1933: 6.

Lane, Maggie. *Jane Austen and Food.* London: Hambledon, 1995.

Lawrence, Margaret. "Sophisticated Ladies." *School of Femininity.* Port Washington: Kennikat, 1936.

Lejeune, C. A. "Angela Thirkell." *Time and Tide* 9 June 1956: 685.

Lerman, Leo. Rev. of *High Rising*, by Angela Thirkell. *Saturday Review of Literature* 31 Oct. 1942: 25:15.

Linn, Thomas. Rev. of *Cheerfulness Breaks In*, by Angela Thirkell. *New York Times* VI 25 Feb. 1941: 2:1.

Mac Liammoir, Michael. Foreword. *Miss Mapp.* By E. F. Benson. London: Heinemann, 1970.

———. Foreword. *Trouble for Lucia*. By E. F. Benson. London: Heinemann, 1968.

Mallet, Isabelle. Rev. of *Growing Up*, by Angela Thirkell. *New York Times* VII 13 Feb. 1944: 3:1.

———. Rev. of *The Headmistress*, by Angela Thirkell. *New York Times* VII 14 Jan. 1945: 5:2.

———. Rev. of *Miss Bunting*, by Angela Thirkell. *New York Times* VII 17 Feb. 1946: 7:2.

Rev. of *Mapp and Lucia*, by E. F. Benson. *Literary Digest* 18 Sept. 1920. 101. *Twentieth Century Literary Criticism* 27. Ed. Dennis Poupard. Detroit: Gale Research, 1988. 1.

Rev. of *Mapp and Lucia*, by E. F. Benson. *New York Times* VII 25 May 1986: 24.

Rev. of *Marling Hall*, by Angela Thirkell. *Commonweal* 23 Oct. 1942: 37:19.

McCullen, Maurice. *E. M. Delafield*. Boston: Twayne, 1985.

McDowell, Margaret. "'E. M. Delafield,' British Novelists, 1890–1928: Traditionalists." *Dictionary of Literary Biography* 34. Ed. Thomas F. Staley. Detroit: Bruccoli, 1985. 90–97.

McInnes, Graham. *The Road to Gundegai*. London: Hogarth, 1985.

Rev. of *Miss Mapp*, by E. F. Benson. *New York Times Book Review* 4 Feb. 1923: 24.

Mitford, Nancy. Introduction. *Make Way for Lucia*. By E. F. Benson. New York: Crowell, 1977.

Mudrick, Marvin. "Irony as Discrimination: *Pride and Prejudice.*" *Jane Austen: A Collection of Critical Essays*. Ed. Ian Watt. Englewood Cliffs: Prentice, 1963.

Nemy, Enid. "Maneuvering in Lucia's Footsteps." *New York Times* XX 18 Feb. 1990: 37.

O'Brien, Kate. Foreword. *The Provincial Lady*. By E. M. Delafield. London: Macmillan, 1947.

Page, Norman. "The Great Tradition Revisited." *Jane Austen's Achievement*. Ed. Juliet McMaster. New York: Harper, 1976.

Parrish, Anne. Foreword. *All About Lucia*. By E. F. Benson. Garden City: Doubleday, 1936.

Patterson, Isabel. Rev. of *The Diary of a Provincial Lady*, by E. M. Delafield. *New York Herald Tribune Books* 4 Oct. 1931: 3.

———. Rev. of *The Provincial Lady in London*, by E. M. Delafield. *New York Herald Tribune Books* 22 Jan.1933: 4.

Pile, Stephen. Introduction. *Mrs. Ames*. By E. F. Benson. London: Hogarth, 1985.

Prescott, Orville. Rev. of *The Headmistress*, by Angela Thirkell. *New York Times* VI 22 Jan. 1945: 15:2.

Priestley, J. B. *The English Comic Character*. London: Bodley, 1925.

———. *English Humour*. New York: Stein, 1976.

Pritchett, V. S. "E. F. Benson: Fairy Tales." *The Tale Bearers*. New York: Random, 1980.

Pym, Barbara. "Home Front Novel." *Civil to Strangers and other Writings*. Ed. Hazel Holt. New York: New American, 1989. 217–269.

Rev. of *Queen Lucia*, by E. F. Benson. *Literary Digest* 18 Sept. 1920: 101.

Read, Miss (Dora Jessie Saint). *No Holly for Miss Quinn*. London: Joseph, 1976.

———. *Village Diary*. London: Joseph, 1957.

Reavell, Cynthia and Tony Reavell. *E. F. Benson: Mr Benson Remembered in Rye, and the World of Tilling*. London: Headley, Invicta, 1984.

Rhondda, Vicountess Margaret (Margaret Thomas). "E. M. Delafield." *Time and Tide* 13 Dec. 1947: 1346.

Roberts, R. Ellis. Obituary, E. F. Benson. *New York Times* 19 Oct. 1940: 19-20.

Seldes, Gilbert. Introduction. *All About Lucia*. By E. F. Benson. Garden City: Doubleday, 1936.

Sherman, Beatrice. Rev. of *August Folly*, by Angela Thirkell. *New York Times* VII 3 Mar. 1937: 18:4.

——. Rev. of *Marling Hall*, by Angela Thirkell. *New York Times* VI 4 Oct. 1942: 14:5.

Southam, B.C. *Jane Austen: The Critical Heritage*, vol. 2. New York: Routledge, 1987.

Southron, Jane Spence. Rev. of *Cheerfulness Breaks In*, by Angela Thirkell. *New York Times* VI 2 Mar. 1941: 7:1.

——. Rev. of *The Provincial Lady in Wartime*, by E. M. Delafield. *New York Times* VI 7 Apr. 1940: 9.

Spacks, Patricia Meyer. *Gossip*. New York: Knopf, 1985.

Strickland, Margot. *Angela Thirkell: Portrait of a Lady Novelist*. London: Duckworth, 1977.

Struther, Jan. *Mrs. Miniver*. 1940. New York: Harcourt, Pocketbook, 1942.

Tanner, Tony. *Jane Austen*. Cambridge: Harvard UP, 1986.

Thompson, Ralph. Rev. of *Before Lunch*, by Angela Thirkell. *New York Times* V 9 June 1940: 21:3.

——. Rev. of *The Brandons*, by Angela Thirkell. *New York Times* VI 26 June 1939: 13:4.

Turner, E. S. *The Phoney War*. New York: St. Martin's, 1962.

Updike, John. "Books." *The New Yorker* 30 Aug. 1990: 86.

Waugh, Auberon. Rev. of *Make Way for Lucia*, by E. F. Benson. *New York Times* VI 7 Aug. 1977: 1.

West, Rebecca. *Ending in Earnest: A Literary Log.* Garden City: Doubleday, 1931.

Woolf, Virginia. "Jane Austen." *The Common Reader.* New York: Harvest, 1953.

———. *The Diary of Virginia Woolf.* IV (1931–1935). Ed. Anne Olivier Bell. London: Hogarth, 1982. 278.

———. *The Diary of Virginia Woolf.* V (1936–1941). Ed. Anne Olivier Bell. London: Hogarth, 1984. 52.

Wright, Edgar. *Mrs. Gaskell: The Basis for Reassessment.* London: Oxford UP, 1965.

Index